IN DANGER'S HOUR

'Convoy'

IN DANGER'S HOUR

by

GORDON HOLMAN

A great ship asks deep waters.
—GEORGE HERBERT

London
HODDER AND STOUGHTON LIMITED

FIRST PRINTED   1948

*Printed in Great Britain for Hodder & Stoughton Ltd., London
by Ebenezer Baylis & Son, Ltd., The Trinity Press, Worcester
and London*

CONTENTS

LIST OF ILLUSTRATIONS

Foreword

TRULY MAY IT BE SAID THAT WHERE ALL ARE OUTSTANDING, TO be outstanding is to be commonplace, and Mr. Holman's simple yet brilliant and moving account of some adventures and encounters up and down the seas, during six years of war, of a magnificent body of men and the ships in which they served—shows them to be outstanding in very truth.

Although many people may not have realised it until the summer of 1940, we were fighting for our lives from the very moment war was declared in September, 1939. It was then that the test—the most terrible test ever applied to a non-fighting service—commenced for the Merchant Navy. Yet to-day, when we know how desperate was our plight at the time of Dunkirk, at the time of the Battle of Britain, at the time of the heavy Blitzes and at the time of Rommel's sweep forward in North Africa, few people ever consider what the outcome would have been if the Merchant Navy had failed. Heroism may have been taken for granted but, at least, the faith of our people in the Merchant Navy was implicit. The trust of this and other Nations was not misplaced.

The war is successfully over and Peace is here, but the work of the Merchant Navy goes on, and is no less vital now than it was in more perilous days, for on it still depends the very existence of this country—our food, the raw materials for our industries and the export of the product of those industries, by which alone can we earn the necessities of life.

The men who maintain the immense traffic of our long seaborne lines of supply made every kind of sacrifice and never

FOREWORD

faltered in time of war, and they do not falter now. This book
is a tribute to their unbreakable courage, and those who read it
will, I feel sure, share the feelings of deep pride, affection and
gratitude with which I commend it to their attention.

Rothermere

Chapter One

Three Hundred Miles off Finisterre

In these anxious days I would like to express to all officers and men in the British Merchant Navy and the British fishing fleets my confidence in their unflinching determination to play their vital part in defence. To each one I would say: Yours is a task no less essential to my people's existence than that allotted to the Navy, Army and Air Force. Upon you the nation depends for much of its foodstuffs and raw materials and for the transport of its troops overseas. You have a long and glorious history, and I am proud to bear the title "Master of the Merchant Navy and Fishing Fleets." I know that you will carry out your duties with resolution and with fortitude, and that the high chivalrous traditions of your calling are safe in your hands. God keep you and prosper you in your great task.

H.M. THE KING'S MESSAGE, SEPTEMBER, 1939

FROM THE CLYDE, BIRTHPLACE OF SO MANY STOUT SHIPS, A British merchantman sailed on her maiden voyage in the late summer of 1938. She sailed south through the hazy seas, was tested by the heat of the Equator, and eventually came to the Cape ports. For such eyes as were there to see, she offered no novelty at any point of her long voyage. She followed a Red Ensign highway.

No doubt she was admired in her ports of call, but, at the same time, those associated with the sea, realised her severely useful purpose. And when she sailed again they were not surprised to see her turn away from the homeward run and set a course for Australia, 5,000 miles further on. That is the way of British ships—to serve by sailing—and sailing home is only incidental to the service.

So the *Clan Forbes*, 7,529 tons gross, with a speed of sixteen knots, carried on across the vast stretch of the Indian Ocean, bent on delivering and collecting merchandise. Weeks later, with 10,000 tons deadweight of cargo, she turned for home, and when she arrived in the Clyde it was ten months, almost to the day, from the time she went away. *Three months still remained before WAR came to Britain.*

In a little more than a fortnight, Captain A. B. Lyall, who had sailed the *Clan Forbes* across the world, took his ship to sea again. Durban, Beira, Mombasa and Mauritius all saw the new vessel before she arrived at Cape Town for the second time. Momentous events were taking place in the world, and the *Clan Forbes* returned to Cape Town as a runner comes to the starting line after limbering up on the track. The ominous crack of the starter's pistol came while she was still there. *On the day after Captain Lyall and his men heard that Britain was at war with Germany, the* Clan Forbes *sailed.*

Those who saw her off, and those who sailed in her, knew that she had more than the normal hazards of the sea to face on the long homeward trip. Already, after a few brief months of peaceful sailing, the "new ship from the Clyde" was a valuable link in Britain's lifeline. Few seamen doubted, even in those first hours of the war, that Nazi Germany would attack that line even more ruthlessly than the Kaiser's Germany had done a quarter of a century earlier.

And so it proved. But the *Clan Forbes* arrived safely in a blacked-out home port just six weeks later.

Sixty years before the *Clan Forbes* made her maiden voyage, a British shipping company was founded which was to play a vital part in two wars of world-wide dimensions. With two ships, amounting to 4,163 gross tons, the Clan Line came into being. It grew rapidly and, by the turn of the century, "Clan Line Steamers" controlled forty-five ships, totalling over 150,000 tons.

More than another 100,000 tons had been added before the outbreak of the First World War, and despite heavy losses between August, 1914 and November, 1918, the Clan tonnage continued to grow, so that when war came again, it was in excess of 300,000 gross tons. Associated with this great shipping undertaking, and also managed by the firm of Cayzer, Irvine and Co., Ltd., were the Houston and Scottish Shire Lines, adding between them nearly another 100,000 tons to the 1939 total. As world carriers, supplying a crowded island which the enemy was to spend years trying to starve into surrender, the sixty cargo liners of these fleets were at once in the "front line".

Forgetful of events at sea, there are those who still speak of "the phoney war" that went on until the May of 1940. It was anything but that for the officers and men who served in these British merchantmen.

In following the fates of these ships, and in telling of the gallantry of their crews, no attempt will be made to dwell on the ordeals and sacrifices that the British Merchant Navy accepted as a whole in the name of duty, and in the cause of their country. But the picture must be painted true to life and, as we know now, the shadows only emphasise the bright glory of achievement and ultimate victory.

Two days before the *Clan Forbes* made her first war-time home-coming, the destructive shadow of the U-boat had made its first appearance among the company of ships to which she belonged. Three hundred miles off Cape Finisterre, in the darkness of the early evening of October 17, 1939, two torpedoes struck home in quick succession on the starboard side of the *Clan Chisholm*. In seven minutes the first of the Clan ships to be the victim of enemy action in the Second World War had disappeared beneath the grey waters of the Atlantic.

The *Clan Chisholm* was on her way home from India and Ceylon with a full cargo. Capable of a good fifteen knots, she steamed independently as far as Port Said. Then, for the first time, she came into the vast Allied convoy network that was to spread across the world. On the evening of Friday, October 13—a combination of day and date not much appreciated by sailors—the *Clan Chisholm* left Gibraltar in a nine-and-half knot convoy on the last lap of her long journey. For four days nothing happened to support those of a superstitious turn of mind, but then, on the 17th, their forebodings were amply justified.

In the afternoon of that day, the ship in which the Commodore of Convoy sailed was torpedoed. Following instructions which he had been given at Gibraltar, Captain F. J. Stenson at once increased to full speed in the *Clan Chisholm* and headed away from the apparent direction of the attack. As the *Clan Chisholm* zig-zagged close to the *Sagaing*, another vessel in the threatened convoy, Captain Stenson made the brief signal: "Propose to make for rendezvous 18th."

The cool efficiency of these Merchant Navy masters brought suddenly face to face with the grim realities of war was reflected in the two-word signal flashed in reply by the *Sagaing*: "I concur."

It was four hours later, when Captain Stenson must have felt confident that he had given the slip to the U-boat which had sunk the Commodore's ship, that two torpedoes hit his vessel. There was no warning before the two under-water explosives crashed home in the engine-room and No. 5 hatch. Captain

"The gun's crew had been left to their fate
as the submarine went under water."

Stenson knew at once that his ship had been mortally wounded. As she began to sink rapidly by the stern, he gave the order: "Abandon Ship."

It is understandable, perhaps, that at this tragic moment when men, who had rightly believed in the security offered by a stout ship, were called upon to abandon her in a very short space of time, there should be some confusion around the boats. The first three boats were got away quickly. Many of the Indian members of the crew were in them, and the boats pulled away from the slanting sides of the *Clan Chisholm*.

Captain Stenson, who had been on his way to collect the ship's papers from his cabin, helped to launch the remaining boat, and as it went down he was pushed into it. Four of the officers and two Indians slid down into the boat after it had reached the water. Although the after deck of the *Clan Chisholm* was awash, the men in the boat waited to see if anyone was left on board to answer their shouts. No answer came, so they pulled for their lives and were not more than sixty yards away when the bows of the *Clan Chisholm* rose high out of the water and then disappeared like a giant shadow of the night.

Then another shadow appeared, picked out by the slight beam of a flash-light. The U-boat had surfaced and the survivors of the British ship, in their tossing boats, knew that they were being sought. It offered them no comfort, and they remained still in their boats until the light went out and the shadow was no longer there.

Next morning, with a north-east wind blowing at Force 5 and a twenty-feet swell running, there appeared one of those scenes which were to become, unhappily, all too familiar in the years that followed. Four boats, each one reminding the others how small they were, alone relieved the grey landscape. Throughout the day, Captain Stenson led them on a course roughly east-south-east. They did not manage to keep together when darkness came down again and, on the third night, a squall gave them added anxiety in their loneliness. One of the engineer officers and several of the native members of the crew were suffering from serious injuries.

For some, but not all of them, succour came next morning, in the shape of the Swedish ship *Bardaland*. The survivors, including Captain Stenson, were landed at Kirkwall on October 24. The Master had to report that the crew of one lifeboat was still missing.

If the enemy thus scored an early point in the long, unbroken battle that went on at sea until peace at last returned to the world, the score was not entirely one-sided. The posters that were begining to appear demanding "security silence", with men's lives as the price to be paid in case of failure, were not fully appreciated by the public, and even seamen themselves were occasionally guilty of talking about forthcoming events.

Additional force was therefore given to a confidential report made by Captain Stenson, and supported by the Masters of at least two other ships that were in the convoy sailing from Gibraltar, that a leakage of information was suspected. Their views were put before the Admiralty, and it may be that the tightening up of security which followed, enabled other ships to escape the fate of the *Clan Chisholm*.

It was also pointed out in confidential documents exchanged at the time, that the convoy system had resulted in the *Clan Chisholm* being bunched with other ships, all limited to the nine-and-a-half knots of the convoy, when she could have proceeded at fifteen knots. The complaint was not so much against the system as the attempt to operate it at a time when we were desperately short of escort vessels. The convoy in question was, in fact, without any form of escort for part of the way.

Here again, good came from evil, because, very early after

the outbreak of hostilities, it was made clear to the Powers-that-be that it was no good looking for safety in numbers and that ships sailing in company might only increase their own risks if they were not given adequate protection. It was the beginning of a controversy that raged all through the early years of the war—whether it was not better for ships with a fair turn of speed to rely on their speed rather than the slight protection offered by one or two escort vessels guarding thirty, forty or fifty ships, all sailing comparatively slowly.

There were those who advocated the building of faster merchant ships—with speeds of eighteen knots or more—and the drastic cutting down of convoys. Arguments against this were that a bottle-neck would be produced in our shipbuilding industry if vessels had to wait for the powerful engines necessary for such speeds, and that there was no guarantee that the enemy would not step-up the speed of U-boats and extend his field of air attack.

In time, he succeeded in doing both these things, but by then, those who had stood firmly for the convoy system, were being vindicated. With men like the late Captain F. J. Walker, R.N., to lead the Navy's vastly-increased forces of U-boat hunters, combined with the powerful aid provided by both R.A.F. long-range aircraft and naval planes flying from carriers sailing with the convoys, the scientific advances of the enemy were more than met, and ships in convoy sailed with increasing security. Still, those who argued in favour of speed could always point to the great liners, such as the *Queen Elizabeth* and *Queen Mary*, who flitted unescorted and unharmed through the very waters which the Germans claimed as U-boat infested.

Twenty-four hours after the sinking of the *Clan Chisholm*, one of her sisters came into the periscope sights of a German submarine commander. She was the *Clan Macbean*, a 5,000-ton ship built at the end of the First World War. Also sailing from Gibraltar, the *Clan Macbean* was proceeding independently, following the scattering of a convoy, and was close enough to the vicinity of the attack on the *Clan Chisholm* to make it more than a possibility that the same U-boat was concerned in both pieces of sea outlawry. And this time the outcome was very different, although the British ship, in the first case, was subject to the same cowardly, hidden assault. The Chief Officer, Mr. H. R. Crosscombe, was on watch at about 7 p.m. on October 18, when he saw a torpedo coming directly towards the *Clan Macbean* from a position two points on the port bow. He immediately put the helm hard over and, as the ship turned, the torpedo went by, missing the bows by little more than inches.

A keen look-out and a quick, seaman-like reaction to danger had beaten the underwater attack, but the modest merchant-man had more to face. Realising that his torpedoes had missed their mark, the U-boat commander surfaced his craft and prepared to carry out by gunfire what he had failed to do with his main armament.

But there he reckoned without the stout hearts of Captain E. Coultas, Master of the *Clan Macbean*, and his British and Indian crew. The U-boat, more mobile on the surface, attempted to get into a position on the quarter of the merchantman. Captain Coultas, however, had no intention of allowing his ship to become a fine big target for the Nazi marksmen. The more the submarine moved round, the more he altered course. With the limited target offered by a constant bows-on view, the Germans held their fire. Although Captain Coultas knew that such a course meant that his own bridge became the bull's-eye for the enemy gunners, he continued to steam straight towards his attackers. That there was method as well as courage in his action was proved when he got to within 200 yards of the submarine. Three quickly-fired shells screamed harmlessly over the *Clan Macbean* and then the aggressor realised that only the most ruthless action could save his craft from destruction. With the sturdy bows of the Red Ensign ship only one hundred feet away, the U-boat commander gave the order to submerge.

As the *Clan Macbean* steamed right over the spot where the submarine had been only minutes before, the cries of the gun's crew who had been left to their fate as the submarine went under water, came up to the ears of the men they had sought to destroy. The Germans, and one Indian member of the crew of the *Clan Macbean* who went overboard in the excitement, may have survived because the U-boat was seen to surface a long way astern of the merchant ship.

The Indian was lost overboard while the boats of the *Clan Macbean* were being lowered to the level of the bulwark rail— a very reasonable precaution in view of the one-sidedness of the conflict. One of the boats up-ended and the Indian, who was already in it, was thrown into the sea.

It is not given to every man to have the dauntless spirit of a Captain Coultas, and there were many men who fought ships with the utmost bravery when *in sight* of the enemy, who told me during the war of their boundless admiration for those who took part in action at sea with no more knowledge of what was going on than was conveyed by the engine-room telegraphs and the ominous, vibratory thud on the keel of underwater explosions. Nowhere more than in ships are the heroes of the engineering and stoking branches appreciated.

There was one such in the *Clan Macbean*. When the call to boat stations went forth, the native crew on duty in the engine-room, possibly by mistake, went to the boats. Second Engineer R. W. C. Bainbridge found himself almost alone. Orders were still coming from the bridge, and they had to be obeyed. The

"Second" remained at his post—and who can say what chances of survival the *Clan Macbean* would have had if his devotion to duty had been on a lesser plane?

The ship arrived safely in the Mersey on October 23 and the Master, reporting this to the owners, did not fail to go through the usual routine of including deck abstracts of Log for passage from Gibraltar to Liverpool, Steaming Statement for same and "a Report *re* Chipping, Scaling and Painting carried out below decks during the voyage".

The Trades Division of the Admiralty pursued Captain Coultas to his home with a complaint about station-keeping. Perhaps they had not heard of his gallantry in face of the U-boat attack, and, in any case, they had their work to do in tightening up the immense convoy system. The fact remains, however, that the first letter the Captain was called upon to write after making his report on the eventful voyage, was one defending himself and his ship.

Having dryly pointed out that "being the slowest vessel in the convoy we were not unnaturally singled out for observation", the Master of the *Clan Macbean* went on to explain that he had given the speed of his ship after consultation with the Chief Engineer. They could make the convoy speed but there was nothing to spare. When they had to alter course to avoid collision with vessels that were not keeping station, the *Clan Macbean* could only get back to her proper place by steaming on a straight course and not zig-zagging. The average speed of the convoy from Port Said to Gibraltar had worked out at slightly more than nine-and-a-half knots, the speed given by Captain Coultas for the *Clan Macbean*.

The hardest heart at the Admiralty must have been softened by the Master's final piece of information. "I may add," he wrote, "that when we were attacked by enemy craft and engines were driven to the very utmost, we did not average more than ten knots; therefore I must assume that the vessel's bottom must be foul."

It was not long before that wonderful band of distinguished sailors—most of them veterans—who came forward to act as Commodores of Convoys, without regard for their own rank and seniority, were expressing their appreciation of the ships of the Merchant Service in which they sailed.

Only three months after the war started, a famous naval leader, Admiral Featherstonehaugh, wrote to the owners of the *Clan Macpherson*:

"Gentlemen, I should like to write to your Company to say how much I appreciated all the kindness and hospitality which I received on board the S.S. *Clan Macpherson*, Mr. H. Cater, Master. The Captain and Officers were most efficient in all the duties appertaining to convoy work, and it was a great pleasure to me to be able to do my work in such a smart and comfortable ship. I must also take this opportunity of mentioning the S.S. *Clan Macilwraith*, who was next ship to me coming from Port Said. She was easily the best station-keeper and signalling ship in the whole convoy of fifty-four ships, and I ventured to make a signal to her to tell her so."

The very next voyage of the *Clan Macpherson* produced further praise, Rear-Admiral J. Hamilton writing of the efficiency with which she carried out the duties of Commodore's ship. He added: "The Captain, Officers and all concerned were most helpful and did everything possible to assist me, and to make my own and my staff's stay as agreeable and pleasant as they could, I am afraid somewhat to their own discomfort. Mr. Bonney, Second Mate, proved a very good navigator."

The *Clan Murdoch* also received the Admiral's approbation, and he concluded: "I can only hope it may be my good fortune to sail in the future in your ships." So the link of good fellowship was forged between the Merchant Service and those who had gladly come into line with it, although their own up-bringing and tradition was almost entirely naval. There may have been a time when the term "Navy type" used by those serving under the Red Ensign was not altogether complimen-tary. The Commodores of Convoys and the Senior Officers of Escort Forces, who rubbed shoulders with the Masters of our merchant ships, and whose methods were subject to the critical eyes of those fine sailors, did much to change the relationship. Polished or rough, it was the capacity to do the job that counted in those days of stress, and both sides learned to respect and admire each other's ability.

The dangers of home waters were emphasised by the loss of the *Clan Morrison* in the latter half of February, 1940. The ship was sailing in ballast from Southampton to Blyth. Wind and weather were moderate and she was proceeding according to Admiralty instructions when a heavy explosion wrecked the vessel. The explosion occurred suddenly in broad daylight when the *Clan Morrison* was eleven miles south of the Cromer Knoll lightship, a favourite area for nocturnal mining opera-tions by the enemy at various periods during the war. Nothing could be done to save the ship and the Master and crew took to the boats. They were later picked up by one of H.M. ships and landed at Grimsby.

In addition to the enemy, the normal hazards of the sea still took their toll. A victim in March, 1940, was the *Clan Stuart*, which sank in the Channel, fortunately without loss of life. She was in a convoy that ran into thick fog. Speed was reduced to seven knots when visibility became so bad that station could only be kept by the use of fog buoys. Late in the afternoon, the lookouts in the *Clan Stuart* had a one-minute view of a vessel heading in from about three points on the starboard bow. Then there was a collision and the other ship, which had not been identified, slipped away into the all-enveloping fog.

Reports made to the Master, Captain Basil Vernon-Browne, by the Chief and Third Officers, after a rapid inspection, left him in no doubt that his ship had been grievously stricken. Water could be heard pouring into No. 2 hatch and, although pumps were started immediately and orders given to close watertight doors, bilge soundings showed ten feet of water. In five minutes this had increased another four feet, and the ship was listing to starboard. In a few more minutes water was rushing from the stokehold into the engine-room. Twenty minutes after the collision, Captain Vernon-Browne gave his last orders in the *Clan Stuart*—"Finished with engines" and "Abandon Ship." In the boats, the crew saw the glow of fire through the cold greyness that was all around them. They saw it spread aft and heard ammunition exploding. Then there was a big explosion and the *Clan Stuart* sank.

The survivors were picked up the same night by the French trawler *Notre Dame de Montlignon*, and later arrived safely in Plymouth.

.   .   .   .   .

Ten days after this unhappy event, the *Clan Forbes* sailed safely home on the completion of her third voyage. She had been away for five months. Her outward voyage had taken her to Durban, Lourenço Marques, Beira and on to Australia. Steaming back across the world, she had called at Singapore, Colombo, Port Said, Gibraltar and Dakar. She had paid her last visit to Dakar for a long time to come.

Chapter Two

Dunkirk and the Tight Blockade

There was the consciousness of silent endurance,
so dear to every Englishman—of standing out against
something, and not giving in.

THOMAS HUGHES

IN THE SPRING OF 1940 THE WAR WAS VERY CLOSE TO OUR SHORES,
and it was to come even closer. The familiar waters which
meant "home" to our sailors coming from all quarters of the
globe, became a hunting-ground for the hidden enemy. Overhead, too, the chances were that aircraft, suddenly arriving,
would bear the black, crooked cross of Nazi Germany.

On a night late in April, Captain Mackinlay, bringing the
Clan Macdonald into Liverpool, sighted a submarine when he
was between Holyhead and the Bar. The submarine submerged, and Captain Mackinlay went on his way wondering
whether it was a U-boat or one of our own craft. He reported
it when picking up his pilot, and the Navy, who had no doubts
on the matter, sent one or two of our all-too-few destroyers
to hunt the enemy at our gate.

Less than a month later, the Germans were pouring into
Holland, France and Belgium, and then "Dunkirk" was the
word on all lips. On May 27, the *Clan Macalister* loaded landing-craft at Southampton. Accommodation was found for
three officers and forty-five naval ratings and the ship arrived
in the Downs late the same evening. At midnight a naval

24

officer climbed on board with orders from the Admiralty. They were addressed to the Master, Captain R. W. Mackie, and Captain Cassidie, R.N., in command of the naval party. The *Clan Macalister* was to proceed at once to a point as near Dunkirk as possible and there discharge the A.L.C.s and their crews. The verbal orders also suggested that Master Mariner and R.N. Captain might make a rendezvous to which damaged landing-craft could return for repairs.

Captain Mackie was given a route through the Downs and the positions of some dangerous wrecks.

When the messenger had departed, Captain Mackie considered the situation. He had a fine ship, nearly 7,000 tons and less than ten years old, which he was asked to take through a wreck-strewn anchorage which had the added hazard of a number of blacked-out ships awaiting their orders. With Captain Cassidie he marked out the route on the chart and dotted in the dangerous wrecks.

Then, his native caution and pride of command asserting itself, he told the four-ring naval officer: "I do not like the job in the dark. We should have a pilot."

Perhaps the naval officer knew more than the Scottish Master because his reply was short and straight to the point. "If you don't like to go, Captain, give me a course to steer, put the boats in the water and I will take them across," he said. To one of a race whose courage is as renowned as its caution, this was challenge enough. By 1 a.m. the *Clan Macalister* had started on her last memorable voyage.

During the night, as they headed towards the Kaempfe Buoy, the radio picked up an SOS.—"unknown steamer torpedoed at Kaempfe Buoy." Captain Mackie, with the bit between his teeth, asked permission of a Patrol vessel to steam straight for Dunkirk across an area marked on his chart "Forbidden to anchor". Permission was not forthcoming. Said

Captain Cassidie grimly: "Take me as close as you can, Captain, discharge my craft and then go back home." The Master of the *Clan Macalister* said nothing.

By 9 a.m. they were in Dunkirk East Roads, receiving orders from various naval vessels, all of which were over-ridden by Captain Cassidie who was determined to get his craft in at all costs. Two A.L.C.s were damaged when a destroyer raced past and caused the merchant ship to roll heavily, but Captain Cassidie headed away with his six sound craft, and then, and only then, did Captain Mackie consider his own position.

He made a mild signal to a destroyer: embarking troops inshore: "Have you any fresh orders for me?" The reply came: "Carry out your original orders." Now that, in view of Captain Cassidie's last instruction, could easily have meant "Go home", but the first gallant human remnants of the little British Expeditionary Force had already managed to scramble on board the *Clan Macalister*. Captain Mackie decided that he had no definite orders, and shifted his anchorage a little further east. More soldiers reached the Clan ship.

From a destroyer came the signal: "Cancel previous orders and await further orders." The *Clan Macalister* was still waiting late in the afternoon when the German bombers came. Like the battle going on on shore, it was a one-sided affair, and when the planes flew off the British merchantman was on fire. Great holes gaped in her deck and men were dying among the twisted girders and wreckage inside the ship. Three bombs had scored direct hits.

Efforts were made to fight the fire, and a destroyer came alongside to help. Wounded men and some of the soldiers, who had had one more bitter experience added to their cup, were transferred to the warship. Then the planes came again and the destroyer had to cast off. By the time the raid was over, the fire had obtained a good hold in the *Clan Macalister*, but Captain

Mackie was still determined to try to put to sea. He was frustrated by a third attack from the air which left him with his telemotor steering gear broken. The fire and exploding ammunition prevented anyone from reaching the hand steering gear aft and it was therefore impossible to get the ship clear of the anchorage. Captain Mackie would have gone aft himself if he had not been prevented by his Chief Officer; and about that time the first of the big shells which had been loaded into the *Macalister* began to explode.

"The enemy were dive-bombing us frequently and we seemed to be a ship marked for destruction," the Master reported later. It was in these circumstances that he called up the engineers, explained the position, and made an appeal for assistance from other ships.

A minesweeper went alongside and, seeing the plight of the merchantman, the Commanding Officer asked Captain Mackie if he wished to abandon his ship. The words stuck in the throat of the Master and it was not until the naval man had compromised with "Temporarily abandon" that Captain Mackie gave the order for the fires to be drawn and for those of his crew who remained to transfer to the sweeper. The *Clan Macalister* burned as part of the great funeral pyre on and off the Dunkirk beaches.

The Germans were not slow to make use of the vast territorial gains which followed hard on the heels of Dunkirk. While England watched and waited for the hour of the expected invasion, the enemy bombers settled on French airfields, and the blockade was soon intensified. Vast areas of sea in which ships had been virtually safe from air attack, were now within their reach.

Heading into the Bay of Biscay, homeward bound on the afternoon of June 24, 1940, the *Clan Ross* was attacked by three Heinkel twin-engined bombers. There was little warning, the planes sweeping down from an overcast sky to machine-gun the decks before returning to drop their bombs. Although struck by the last bomb of the first salvo, the *Clan Ross* stoutly defended herself during the twenty minutes she was under attack.

Officers and engineers of the ship joined the D.E.M.S. gunners, and the Heinkels must have been surprised at the warmth of their reception. Not one man left his post at the 12-pounder H.A. or Lewis guns when the ship was hit. The mixed team on the high-angle gun, led by Gunner Harold Webb, included Third Officer T. R. Halliday, Apprentice C. F. Sims, Fifth Engineer W. J. McCandish and Seaman Gunner R. H. Stewart. The bridge Lewis gun was kept going almost non-stop by Second Officer J. Patterson, and three gunners of the 147th Light A.A. Battery stood in exposed positions to maintain rapid and effective fire with similar weapons.

Captain T. W. Inman kept the ship on a violent zig-zag course, while the Chief Officer, Mr. S. W. Brown, dealt successfully with a fire started by the bomb-hit. The *Clan Ross* was shaken by other bombs which fell near, but, when the planes flew off, her crew were confident that two of them had suffered damage. They themselves had escaped without casualties and their vessel was still seaworthy.

Captain Inman brought his ship safely into Milford Haven where, in reporting the heavy machine-gunning he had experienced from the attacking aircraft, he added: "I beg to submit the suggestion that all defensive armament should be fitted with protection for the crews against this type of attack." He commended his crew for their zeal and coolness in action and the way they had stood up to the strain of that month in particular, when they had "experienced machine-gun fire on three occasions, the blowing up of another vessel by a magnetic mine only a ship's length away, and almost daily air raid alarms."

Sturdy British construction, which helped the *Clan Ross* through her ordeal, was also largely responsible for the survival of the *Clan Ogilvy*, torpedoed in the same area less than a week later. The crew took to the boats after the torpedoing, but two hours later returned to their ship and, with luck on their side in the shape of fine weather and a calm sea, brought her into Falmouth, although gaping holes to port and starboard let both sea and daylight into her No. 1 hold. Again there were no casualties.

Even at this stage of the war, when enemy attacks still held something of novelty, it was not unusual to find Masters more disturbed by mishaps at sea than by the efforts of the Germans. A good instance of this was provided by Captain B. A. Hardinge when the *Clan Murray*, coming south in a North Sea convoy, fouled the Sheringham Light float. In his report to the owners, he described at length how, at about midnight, the convoy of thirty ships ran into another convoy northward bound. For a short time there was confusion as vessels switched on their steaming lights and passed each other, sometimes with only a few feet to spare. Captain Hardinge steered clear of all other shipping and then, for one minute at 00.18 (the time is given precisely), the *Clan Murray* "rubbed" along the Light float. No damage was done to the ship, and the light was afterwards seen to be functioning. Nevertheless the matter was reported by the Captain to the Receiver of Wrecks and Inquiries when he arrived in the Port of London.

Tacked on to this account is a paragraph which reveals that at breakfast-time following the disturbing night encounter with the north-bound convoy, a formation of enemy bombers appeared over the *Clan Murray* and her companion ships. What followed, Captain Hardinge dealt with in one sentence: "They flew the whole length of the convoy dropping salvos of high-explosive bombs, the vessel ahead of our ship was struck and sunk, four bombs straddled us to port and starboard at about ten feet from the sides—one each side of bridge and one each side of quarter—there was considerable shock and concussion and a small amount of damage was done to deck fittings."

And some well-satisfied Hun raiders no doubt returned to their base confident that they had frightened the life out of the British Merchant Navy!

That this true and seamanlike regard for the normal hazards of the sea was not misplaced was proved about this time by the loss of the *Clan Macfarlane*, a 6,000-ton ship, in collision. The disaster occurred on a rough night in the Indian Ocean in an area where ships were required to navigate without lights. The other vessel was only in the view of the *Clan Macfarlane* for two minutes before the collision. Five minutes later the 6,000-ton ship had disappeared and many of her crew were struggling in the water. Even so, there had been no panic among the Europeans or Indians, who had gone to their boat stations with the utmost coolness. The bows of the other ship had sheared away all the port-side lifeboats, and the rough sea prevented the launching of those on the weather side. The other ship, which used her searchlight and then stood by until daylight to search carefully among the floating wreckage, saved many lives. About half the crew, and twenty out of twenty-four Askari soldiers travelling in the ship, were lost.

The next vessel of the fleet to fall victim to a U-boat was the *Clan Menzies*, a ship capable of loading more than 10,000 tons of cargo, which had only been at sea since 1938. It must be remembered that crack U-boat commanders were operating at this time. Later in the war many of them had been eliminated and there came a dilution both in the skill and determination of those commanding U-boats. There was, unfortunately, a

"For a short time there was confusion
as vessels switched on their steaming lights
and passed each other sometimes with
only a few feet to spare"

Commander with deadly skill in the submarine which sighted the *Clan Menzies* off the north-west coast of Ireland on a night at the end of July, 1940.

The *Clan Menzies* had come from Melbourne and was steaming independently. With darkness to cover her, she was making seventeen knots and zig-zagging when a torpedo struck her on the starboard side of the engine-room. It was a mortal wound, and the Master, Captain W. J. Hughes, gave the order to "Abandon Ship." The starboard lifeboats had been turned into matchwood by the explosion and the men crowded into the two remaining boats. To the overloaded boats—there were fifty-one men in one and thirty-seven in the other—the U-boat came. The survivors were required to give information about their ship, their port of loading, their destination and their cargo. Then the U-boat departed, with the warning that if any lights were shown the boats would be shot up. Captain Hughes, who had been prevented from sending an SOS by damage to his wireless equipment caused in the explosion, sailed his boat into a small Irish harbour. Survivors in the second boat were picked up by an Irish ship. Casualties were confined to the two engineers and four native ratings killed in the torpedo explosion.

A valuable cargo of Indian produce was unloaded from the *Clan Monroe* (Captain C. W. Banbury) in the London docks about this time. The ship, still loaded with 1,500 tons of manganese ore, then joined a convoy sailing from Southend. Less than eight hours later, her back was broken by a heavy underwater explosion and twelve of her crew were killed.

It must not be thought, because one records the passing of fine ships in this bitter hour of our long sea history, that the Clan fleet was being crippled. Vessels still continued to come and go in many ports all over the world and supplies continued to arrive in hard-pressed Britain. The *Clan Macbean* docked at

Cardiff after helping with the evacuation of French troops to Casablanca and a number of civilians from Gibraltar. In a few days she was off again, passing safely through the danger belt despite a bombing attack in the Irish Sea. Heading south, she picked up thirty-six survivors of the S.S. *Brookwood* who had been in their boats for five days. Before landing them at Freetown, the *Clan Macbean* offered them the consolation of tobacco to the extent of 8,950 cigarettes.

In August, 1940, there was one more heavy loss, the *Clan Macphee*, almost the oldest ship in the fleet at the outbreak of war, being torpedoed when outward bound from Liverpool to East African ports and Bombay. Survivors from her crew had the unhappy experience of being torpedoed twice before they again reached home.

For three days, the *Clan Macphee* sailed in convoy. Very shortly after the convoy had been dispersed in the North Atlantic, the old ship, which had survived one world war, was torpedoed by a U-boat which had no doubt shadowed the convoy. Only three members of the crew were injured by the explosion, but more than thirty lost their lives when one of the lifeboats became swamped during launching. The *Clan Macphee* sank in eight minutes and with her went her gallant Master, Captain T. P. Granwell.

The survivors were picked up a few hours later by the Hungarian steamer *Kelet*. There were not sufficient stores in the *Kelet* to keep both her crew and the men from the *Clan Macphee* for any length of time, so the Master of the Hungarian vessel decided to make for Fayal. Two days later his ship was also torpedoed. Rescuers and rescued shared boats and rafts for five days before being picked up by a Norwegian ship which took them into Galway.

Early in September, 1940, the *Clan Lamont*, a brand new vessel of over 7,500 tons, arrived safely in port at Hull, her holds full of vitally important merchandise. She had had a narrow escape right at the end of her voyage when attacked by a German bomber. Such were the shortages that faced us, even after twelve months of war, that the *Clan Lamont*, a most valuable ship, had been left almost defenceless. She had been given a high-angle gun, and had then seen it taken away again. The Master, on arrival in Hull, pleaded for its return. And nobody could question his statement when he said: "In the case of ships arriving in home waters and not in convoy, the means of defence against air attack are essential."

.　　　.　　　.　　　.　　　.

Voyage No. 4 of the *Clan Forbes* was completed about this time. Sailing early in April under the command of her new Master, Captain J. D. Elvish, she had made the round trip through the Suez Canal to Colombo, Madras and Calcutta, and home via the Cape. She arrived at Tilbury to discharge the first part of her cargo on July 31, 1940. All through August the *Clan Forbes* provided a "front row in the stalls" for the Battle of Britain. Raids went on day and night, while high in the heavens Spitfires and Hurricanes beat back what was intended to be the first wave of the enemy's great invasion operation. The battle raged in Britain's air, and life for those below was expected to go on more or less normally. The animals and crops had to be attended to on the land, coal had to be won from the Kentish mines, the Army had to strengthen its frontal positions along the coast and ships had to be unloaded.

It was a testing time for all, and how well they stood the test the whole world knows. For a fortnight, the *Clan Forbes*, lit by the red glow of fires night after night, was untouched. Then, at midday on August 15, during a high level attack by German bombers, the big vessel suffered a direct hit on the gun plat-

33

form aft. The gun's crew, under Second Officer Hume and Fourth Officer J. Green, were standing at their gun, ready for action. The bomb went through the gun platform and did not explode until it reached the crew's quarters below. Some of the gun's crew had amazing escapes, but a radio officer, a shore workman and three Indians were killed, and thirteen other members of the crew wounded. Fire broke out but was quickly dealt with, and the ship was not badly damaged.

The *Clan Forbes* remained under the battle for another three weeks, and then sailed in convoy to Middlesbrough to discharge 2,000 tons of pig iron, the remainder of her cargo.

To the Masters of fine ships, such as the *Clan Forbes*, it must have suggested trailing one's coat to be tied to a motley company of ships moving at a less-than-sedate seven knots under the nose of the enemy. "E-Boat Alley" was no place in which to relax, even years later. In 1940, when the Germans, believing final victory was round the corner, had hardly had time to realise the dogged determination of our seamen, it was a good spot to leave behind. But the little ships, "flat irons" taking the vital coal to London and coasters relieving the harassed British railways, needed the protection of the Navy and the R.A.F. as much as the big ships. Our escort forces would not run to fast and slow convoys, any more than the R.A.F. could stretch their limited resources to constant air cover.

In the confined waters where London's river joins the sea, and in the narrower parts of the Channel and the North Sea, the danger was constant. It was "Action stations" all the time, and when, during one passage, I dozed on the desk in the ship's office because all other compartments were sealed off behind closed watertight doors, my "bed" was regarded as the height of luxury in E-Boat Alley travel.

Big ships naturally ran the greater risk because they were liable to become the bull's-eye of the enemy's attacks. In fairness to the smaller vessels, it must be pointed out that they suffered their degree of risk much more frequently. Nor were those who served in them ever lacking in pluck. Indeed, their nonchalance was a constant source of concern to those in command of escort forces and those responsible for ships more used to the wide oceans. Perhaps it was a mixture of irritation and admiration that made Captain Elvish write, after the safe arrival of the *Clan Forbes* at Middlesbrough: "the speed of the convoy (7 knots) and the coasters who were in it and who seemed to obey only their own whims as to position and speed, made the passage an anxious one."

The *Clan Forbes* experienced more air raids while unloading her pig iron at Middlesbrough, but was not involved in any incident and sailed for Methil on September 10. A few days later she was in convoy again, with the Commodore flying his flag in the *Clan Buchanan*, making a north-about run to Newport, Monmouthshire. Although the Commodore was not in his own ship, Captain Elvish made the note: "It is very obvious that all Commodores prefer to be on vessels like our modern ones as they have confidence in the gyro compasses for passages where it is often difficult to check the errors of a magnetic compass."

Once again the dangers of home waters were proved, although the convoy had taken the safer passage to the northward through the Pentland Firth. Just as the convoy was about to disperse at dawn on September 17th, a German bomber swooped in and dropped bombs close to the port column, narrowly missing the *City of Paris*. The convoy was then off the mouth of the Clyde.

At Newport, the *Clan Forbes* went into dry dock and was then taken over to load for a secret destination. It was a short-lived secret. Cargo coming alongside in trucks was clearly marked—"MALTA".

Chapter Three

East and West to Malta

Strive, and hold cheap the strain;
Learn, nor account the pang; dare, never grudge the throe!
ROBERT BROWNING

ODD THINGS BEGAN TO HAPPEN TO THE "CLAN FORBES" AS HER cargo was slowly loaded. Naval officers arrived, and, after a critical survey of the lines of the ship, various measurements were taken. Then a considerable amount of wood and other material appeared on the quay and a small army of carpenters and fitters set to work on the merchantman. They erected strange deck structures, and dummy guns were built into position. Cranes and boats were added and, to cap it all, a good imitation of a second funnel was constructed on the after-end of the boat deck.

The sailors looked at the *Clan Forbes* and suddenly realised that her appearance had been completely changed. Those who knew the depot ship H.M.S. *Maidstone* swore that the merchantman would be the dead spit of her at only a few hundred yards range, once she was at sea. And that was the idea—the *Clan Forbes* was to sail disguised as a Navy ship. In this way she might avoid some of the attention the enemy were bound to give her if they knew she was carrying a full cargo of relief supplies to the island fortress in the Mediterranean.

By the third week in October, the disguise was complete.

Extra guns—the real thing this time—had been placed in the ship and accommodation provided for service gunners. By final dispensation of the Admiral in command of the area, the *Clan Forbes* sailed under the White Ensign. ("This must have been one of the very few occasions that this privilege has been granted to a ship that was not under the command of a Commissioned Officer of His Majesty's Royal Navy," Captain Elvish noted, with justifiable pride.)

The *Clan Forbes* first sailed north to the Clyde. On November 15, in company with the *Clan Fraser* and the Cunard liner *Franconia*, she left, having taken on board a number of naval personnel for signal duties. A strong escort was replaced next morning by an even stronger ocean escort consisting of the aircraft-carrier *Furious*, three cruisers and a destroyer screen. Signals began to pass between the flagship of the force and the other vessels, and Captain Elvish found that he was expected to take part in various fleet manœuvres. The Merchant Navy ships were being drilled for the big test ahead.

Two days of bad weather had little effect on the force, beyond exposing a few of the weaknesses in the *Clan Forbes'* disguise. The dummy funnel, in particular, suffered, and the planks from which it was made began to open up so that daylight could be seen through it. This was of little consequence because, before the ships entered the Straits of Gibraltar, the Navy decided against the disguise and asked Captain Elvish to do his best to dismantle it. It was no easy task, however, and the *Clan Forbes* entered the Mediterranean still looking more like the *Maidstone* than the *Clan Forbes*.

The *Furious* and the *Franconia* had gone their respective ways, and it became clear to those in the two Clan ships that they had been chosen to take part in the first west to east supply convoy to run to Malta since the entry of Italy into the war. They recognised the dangers of their task, and they

37

appreciated the honour of having been picked to carry it out.

A midnight passage through the Straits took them well into the Western Mediterranean before daybreak. As the sun rose ahead of them, the Merchant Navy men saw that they were in new and impressive company. There, solid and reassuring, was the *Ark Royal*—which the Germans weeks before had even pictured in their newspapers as sinking—and, spreading out ahead and around the convoy, the battle-cruiser *Renown*, H.M.S. *Sheffield* and three other cruisers, a number of sloops and a screen of destroyers. Whatever might be ahead, it was a stirring moment that not one man in the two Clan ships would have wished to miss.

A destroyer slipped in close to the *Clan Forbes* and, by means of a Coston gun and line, "fired" a set of orders on to the merchant ship. These left no doubt that, in company with the Navy's famous "Force 'H' ", she, and the *Clan Fraser*, were making for Malta. They were, in fact, taking part in "Operation Collar", and Admiral Sir James Somerville set this out in the following "Information for Ships' Companies after leaving harbour":

"The object of the present operation is to pass reinforcements of ships, men and material through to the Eastern Mediterranean and to escort back certain ships from there to Gibraltar.

"The operation is on a larger scale than anything we have attempted hitherto, but I see no reason why it should not be completely successful.

"Success, however, depends on every officer and man realising to the full his personal responsibility in this operation, and determining that there shall be no lack of vigilance or attention to duty on his part. We shall do our best to avoid being seen by the enemy. Puffs of smoke from the funnels or 'Charley Noble' [galley funnels], or lights carelessly exposed at night, may disclose our position and must be carefully guarded against.

"If we meet with equal or inferior enemy forces, we shall fight our way through. If superior forces are encountered, we may have to mark time until reinforced by the Mediterranean Fleet, because our movements are hampered to some extent by the transports we are escorting.

"One of these transports [the *Clan Forbes*] may look a bit odd, and you may wonder what she is. Perhaps she is Winston's Secret Weapon; perhaps she is not. Whatever she is, or may be, say nothing about her. Where we have been and what we have done is *our* business and no one else's. Up-to-date, we have been most successful in keeping our movements and actions concealed. I attribute this largely to the loyal co-operation of officers and men in preserving strict secrecy before and especially *after* operations are completed."

The "Secret Weapon", doing a spritely sixteen knots and perhaps a little self-conscious, took up her position. The *Clan Fraser*, under her Master, Captain Herbert J. Giles, kept her company. Two days passed fairly quietly, but early on November 27 the first hostile aircraft appeared. They were met by fighter aircraft from the *Ark Royal*, but very shortly after the air threat had been dealt with, there came word to the merchantmen that the Italian Fleet was at sea. With a destroyer escort, the Clans were instructed to alter course to the south. More air attacks developed, and a submarine was located as the all-important supply ships steered towards the African coast. The destroyers dealt with the submarine, and the two Clans turned again to head towards their destination.

Much has already been written about the naval action that was taking place at this time to the northward. Perhaps for purposes of this book it is best summed up in the words of Captain Elvish in his report: "This action afterwards became known as the Battle of Spartivento, but it was not much of a battle as only our ships wanted to fight."

At nightfall, the merchant vessels, which included the *New Zealand Star* going on to Alexandria, took leave of Force "H", and, with only a destroyer escort, made a dash through the Pantellaria channel. Next morning they made contact with units of the main Mediterranean Fleet. They, too, departed later in the day, and the enemy made one last desperate effort to prevent the sea-borne supplies reaching Malta. Aeroplanes came over and bombs dropped all round the merchant ships so that the *Clan Fraser* appeared to be hit, but, to the relief of those in the *Clan Forbes*, she steamed out of the cascades of water unharmed. Both ships entered Grand Harbour to the cheers of the hard-pressed islanders and the strains of a Royal Marine band in a cruiser playing "A Life on the Ocean Waves".

Relief had come to Malta in no uncertain way. Four other merchant ships that had made the run from the eastern end of the Mediterranean, were already in the harbour. For the Clan Line it was indeed a proud moment. Five of the six ships flew their house flag, the other three being the *Lanarkshire*, the *Clan Ferguson* and the *Clan Macaulay*.

They remained in Grand Harbour for three weeks while supplies of every description were unloaded. Then, on December 21, the *Clan Forbes* and *Clan Fraser* started the perilous voyage home, and the other ships steamed to the eastward.

The battleship *Malaya* joined the two vessels on the way to Gibraltar as, with a destroyer screen, they made for the Pantellaria channel. At about 2 a.m. there was an emergency signal from the battleship for the merchantmen to make a double turn to starboard. The order had hardly been carried out when there was a big explosion and it was seen that one of the escort had been torpedoed or had struck a mine. The convoy resumed its original course while who knows what desperate efforts were being made in the few remaining hours of darkness to save men or stricken ship? Once through the Channel, the convoy came under the strong cover of Force "H" again, and this time the Italian Navy did not attempt to interfere with it.

The Clan ships arrived back in Gibraltar harbour on Christmas Eve, and the gallant part played by the Merchant Navy in taking relief to Malta was acknowledged by an invitation to officers to lunch with Admiral Sir James Somerville on Christmas Day. But even on that day of Peace the toasts were cut short by a sudden call to the Navy, H.M.S. *Renown* leading Force "H" to sea to deal with an enemy threat to an inbound convoy.

Two days later, the *Clan Forbes* and *Clan Fraser* sailed independently for the United Kingdom. From the Clyde, where they both arrived safely, Captain Elvish reported on his own crew: "During the whole operation all on board behaved in an exemplary manner and I cannot speak too highly of their conduct. Co-operation from the engineers was of the highest order and the speed asked for by the Navy was always available and was maintained. The behaviour of the Indian members of the crew was excellent . . ."

.   .   .   .   .   .

During the period of the epic run to Malta, other ships of the Clan fleet had gone through a variety of experiences, not all of them pleasant. And here it should be made clear that not every day at sea in war-time was unpleasant. Even the element of danger that was always present in one degree or another, added spice to life for many men who had chosen the sea years before because it was a man's way of living. A grim kind of humour was to be found in most convoys. There was always an "ugly duckling" or a ship that never did the right thing.

In one fast convoy, with which I made an eastward crossing of the Atlantic, there was a ship that not only was too slow, but constantly made smoke. By straggling she imposed a strain on the resources of the escort, and by making smoke she attracted attention that might endanger the whole convoy. Two days out from the American shore, she was ordered to go back and wait for a slower convoy. Reluctantly, rather like a faithful dog that has received an inexplicably harsh order from its master, the old ship dropped behind until she was out of sight over the horizon. But the Convoy Commodore had reckoned without the determination, however wilful, of a British Master. Next morning there was a smudge of smoke astern and then, unbelievably, the offender, who should have been almost back in New York, reappeared, and for a time actually gained on the convoy. This was only made possible, apparently, by great effort on the part of her stokers (the black smoke bore witness) and a complete disregard of the zig-zag being carried out by the convoy.

Remaining at a respectful distance, the disobedient Master "did a Nelson", as the sailors would say, to repeated signals to turn about and leave the convoy. Then it appeared that he had repented, and the old ship once again retired over the horizon. But next morning she was back again, and although strong terms were used in signals to her on subsequent days—to which, as far as I could see, no reply was ever made—she was still hanging on when we arrived home. For some odd reason, hundreds of men in that convoy got a lot of pleasure out of seeing that old ship and her defiant Master show up each morning. In peace we may become docile, but it is no docile spirit that helps us to win wars.

At the end of October, 1940, heavy weather around our shores and in the Atlantic worried Masters quite as much as the U-boats. The *Clan Macnair*, for instance, came in with all her lifeboats except one washed away or smashed. Doors and ladders had also been washed over the side, part of her cargo was damaged and sea-water had contaminated some of her fuel oil.

All these matters were carefully reported by her Master, Captain J. H. Crellin, before he mentioned that, despite the weather, his ship had saved the lives of fourteen survivors of a Greek steamer sunk by aerial bombing.

Enemy bombing, too, accounted for the *Clan Mackinlay*, (Captain R. S. Masters) after she had actually arrived safely in the mouth of the Clyde with a valuable Indian cargo brought *via* the Cape. Re-directed to Methil by the Naval Control, the ship was struck by two bombs when off Noss Head and sank in less than two hours with the loss of five of her crew, including the Chief Engineer, and her important cargo.

The M.V. *Stirlingshire* (Scottish Shire Line) was equally unfortunate, although in her case, happily, there was no loss of life. Sailing from Sydney, New South Wales, with a cargo of frozen meat and general merchandise, she joined up with a convoy from Halifax crossing the Atlantic. She passed through a gale of hurricane force when off the coast of Newfoundland, saw four vessels in the convoy torpedoed during the crossing, and was then torpedoed herself when less than 300 miles from home.

With great difficulty the crew were picked up by the British steamer *Empire Puma*, and Captain C. E. O'Byrne, of the *Stirlingshire*, recorded "the very gallant action" of Captain J. D. Ramsay and his crew, who turned back to make the rescue when "not detailed by convoy instructions to this duty."

Early in 1941, the *Clan Macaulay* made another run into Malta, and had a miraculous escape from destruction while in harbour. There had been a gale on the night of January 17-18, and the Master, Captain A. Campbell, asked next day to be moored in a new berth as his anchors had dragged. Permission was given and the ship was just beginning to move under main steam when an air raid developed. Dive-bombers came down in a concentrated attack, and two heavy bombs crashed into the water just where the *Clan Macaulay* had been moored only a few minutes earlier.

The bombs exploded on striking the water and the ship was still so close at hand that two of the crew were wounded and thirty-seven splinter holes were pierced in the ship's side above the waterline.

"We managed to get a goodly number of shots into the air from our anti-aircraft gun to help singe their tails," the Master reported. And if he could have caught them after he had had the opportunity of examining his paint store, Captain Campbell would probably have done more than singe their tails. A 7-cwt. drum of buff colour paint, a 3-cwt. drum of white paint, two drums of grey paint, two drums of red-lead and a 5 gallon drum of raw linseed oil were all punctured by large splinters, and the natural colour scheme that spread over a wide area was more fantastic than anything ever conceived by the camouflage experts!

Three Clan ships that had been voyaging for four to five months, all arrived home safely at the beginning of February. On the 1st, the *Clan Matheson*, 5,613 gross tons, arrived in London, and on the following day the *Clan Buchanan*, 7,266 tons, and the *Clan Colquhoun*, 7,914 tons, berthed at Liverpool. The combined deadweight capacity of these ships was not far short of 30,000 tons, so one more blow was aimed at Hitler's long-term method of winning the war—by blockade.

Let us follow these three ships, sailing for thousands of miles under the Red Ensign. First away was the *Clan Colquhoun*, twenty years old like the *Matheson*. Her outward run took her to Cape Town, Simonstown, Mossel Bay, Port Elizabeth, East London, Durban, Freemantle, Townsville, Bowen and Sydney.

For the homeward passage, she loaded 2,758 tons of lead and 243 tons of frozen beef at Townsville, 109 tons of frozen beef at Bowen, 187,300 carcases of lamb and mutton, 710 bales of wool and 616 bags of mail at Sydney, and 200 tons of maize meal at Cape Town. Average speed, except for the final run home in convoy from Cape Town, was eleven to twelve knots. And at the end of this trip across the world, Captain A. G. Storkey, Master of the *Clan Colquhoun*, said of his crew: "I have received loyal co-operation from all the officers, engineers and crew during the voyage."

Captain S. Carter took the *Clan Matheson* out of Liverpool nearly three weeks after the *Clan Colquhoun* had sailed. It was not a happy start to a long voyage, heavy weather being encountered at once and two ships being torpedoed when the convoy was only three days out. But thirty days later Cape Town was reached. The second lap of the voyage took the *Clan Matheson* to far-away Cochin, with various ports of call on the way. On the return run, when between Cochin and Durban, there was a fire in the ship. For four hours at night, the whole of the European crew, including gunners, worked to put this out. Christmas was spent with the ship midway between Cape Town and Freetown. In the final run home, Captain Carter, who had tried to get a high-angle gun for his ship both in Glasgow and Liverpool without success, saw German aircraft pick on unprotected vessels, one of which was sunk and another set on fire. "I am convinced (he reported) that these ships would not have been hit if they had been provided with H.A. guns, as the planes immediately sheered off when fired upon."

Clan Buchanan, youngster of the trio, having been built in 1938, had sailed from this country at the end of September, 1940. She had gone round the Cape and on to India and Ceylon. Back in Liverpool, her Master, Captain D. Davenport Jones, sat down and wrote a one-and-a-half page report to cover the whole voyage. It was pithy as well as brief, as these extracts indicate:

"This voyage there have been no 'events' and all has gone according to plan as routed."

"Coasting in India was normal, and finally left Madras a full ship."

"*Re* engines—no involuntary stops, and only usual voyage repairs required."

"*Re* weather—normal until in Polar regions and then fierce."

"Very unsatisfactory, valuable ship having one rapid-firing rifle as only A.A. defence."

Masters bringing their ships home after long and anxious voyages must have been inclined to wonder on occasions whether they were as welcome as Press and Radio constantly suggested. They can have had no doubts in their hearts, but the difficulties of those particularly trying months, when German bombing was most widespread, often led to odd receptions.

The *Clan Murdoch* arrived in the Clyde towards the end of February, 1941, to complete a round trip of 27,924 miles. Enormous as this mileage may sound, it should be said at once that it was nothing exceptional.

Captain H. S. Booth, Master of the *Clan Murdoch*, has recorded in almost comic detail what happened to his ship after her arrival. Two of his boats had been carried away by very heavy weather off the Azores and the immediate result of this was that the *Clan Murdoch* had to wait eight days in the Clyde for replacements. She then sailed as Commodore ship in a convoy bound for Methil, only to run into another heavy gale in the Pentland Firth. Fourteen hours were spent in Methil and

"There, solid and reassuring
was the "Ark Royal.""

then the ship was ordered to the Tyne. Arriving off the Tyne, Captain Booth was informed that he must proceed to the Tees as the Tyne was closed. When his ship was two miles off the Tees, he heard that the Tees was also closed and that he was to make for the Humber. Arriving there, he anchored off the Humber Light vessel and, after a few hours, found that the *Clan Murdoch* had become the target of a German raider.

It proved to be nothing more than an exciting interlude and, when it was over, officers and men settled down to wait for next day's orders. They came on the following afternoon, when an Examination vessel appeared and passed the message that the Humber was open and the *Clan Murdoch* was to follow them in. Up came the anchor, and Captain Booth dutifully followed the little vessel, only pausing for a moment to pick up the Pilot off Spurn Head.

Getting the Pilot on board was like tempting fate. Another Examination vessel arrived alongside the big merchantman and, countermanding the orders of the first, informed Captain Booth that the Admiralty required him to return to the Tyne to discharge. Twenty-four hours later, the *Clan Murdoch* anchored three miles off the entrance to the Tyne in a snowstorm, which lasted for another twenty-four hours.

Then, when Captain Booth may have thought the joke was getting a little worn—he did not record his feelings—one more Examination vessel appeared with the information that the Tyne was closed and the *Murdoch* was to proceed back to Methil. Arriving there next day, Captain Booth decided to try and improve his luck by going ashore himself to see the naval authorities. He was told that he could leave next day for the Tyne, which would be open in forty-eight hours. A few hours later there came the final change of orders. He was instructed to sail at once for Dundee, where, in due course, the *Clan Murdoch* safely docked.

Fortunately the Merchant Navy had powerful advocates on shore. Lord Rotherwick, Chairman of the Clan Line and a man with a lifetime of experience in shipping to give weight to his words, spoke challengingly when he became President of the Chamber of Shipping of the United Kingdom in this very month of February, 1941. "I recognise," Lord Rotherwick said, "the urgent needs of the Army and Air Force, but it is, in my opinion, vital that equal priority should be given to the supply of armament to merchant ships, in order that no vessel may be left without means of repelling attacks from the air. Our shipping is our lifeline and unless we can maintain the flood of imports from overseas, our fighting Services will be unable to function and our civil population will starve. Next only to defence against invasion, the first and most urgent task to-day is to ensure the safety of our ships."

Stressing the need for making effective use of our tonnage, Lord Rotherwick continued: "Almost as important as its safety is the effective use of our shipping. We should be constantly reviewing this problem in order to ensure that: (1) we are not using fast ships on less dangerous services which could be performed by slow ships; (2) that by this means we reduce the time each ship has to spend in passing through the danger areas and thus reduce the ratio of risk to cargo imported or exported; (3) that we cut to a minimum the delays unavoidable to shipping under war conditions, subject only to the paramount consideration of safety. Ships to-day are sailing fully loaded, quite a novel experience for liners who for years have been sailing half full. Yet much of this increased carrying capacity is wasted by the longer voyages and the delays which occur in port. There is much that must be done to speed up the handling of vessels in port and loading or discharging, in carrying out repairs, or while awaiting convoys, or in sending them on from the port of arrival to their ultimate port of destination in the United Kingdom. Precious days are lost where every day counts for victory. . . ."

Lord Rotherwick not only continued to be watchful of the interests of the Merchant Navy generally, he also permitted his lovely home, Tylney Hall, Hampshire, to become the "headquarters" from which many important ships were operated.

The *Halizones*, of the Houston Line, came home through the heavy storms of the winter of 1940–41, having left these islands in the middle of summer. She had gone out with a load of explosives, her last memory of home waters, after leaving Crossby Sands, being the blacked-out Bar Light Vessel which she passed just before midnight on August 16, 1940. Next day she was in a large convoy, ships having joined from north and south. During the four days that the convoy remained together, the crew of the *Halizones* twice saw ships of the escort alter course to pick up survivors in lifeboats. Although this was not altogether encouraging, it did not prevent the Master (Captain Jack E. Townrow) saying that it was "somewhat of a relief to be on our own," when ships separated.

According to his own record, he turned in a little after midnight, and one is left to assume that it was the first night he had permitted himself this luxury since the *Halizones* sailed. He was wakened at daybreak by the Chief Officer, and heard that it was suspected that a submarine was following them. The gun's crew were quickly at their stations and all eyes were strained to try to pick up the target. There was a good deal of waiting and sighting, and then one round was fired at what was though to be a submarine's periscope.

There were sceptics who declared it was a whale, and their belief was strengthened when a whale was sighted later. But, in the words of the Master: "the shot was a very good one, and I am glad to say that we were not troubled again by submarines, or, for that matter, whales."

49

The *Halizones* crossed the Line on September 4 and encountered strong south-east Trades with a rough head sea, which continued until the ship was one day's run from Cape Point. Then the wind worked round to the south-west, and a very rough following sea and high swell developed. After a call at Durban for bunkering, the *Halizones* pushed on. Keeping up a steady eleven knots, she reached Colombo on October 11. Her arrival caused a minor sensation, another ship reporting her by wireless as a suspected raider as she was passing through the One-and-a-half Degree Channel.

Next leg of the voyage was to Madras, where the ship arrived on the evening of October 19. She anchored, expecting to enter harbour by daylight. The authorities were in a hurry however, and at 2 a.m. orders came to go inside. With difficulty the unlighted buoy was picked up at the entrance to the swept channel and the explosives berth was reached two-and-a-quarter hours later.

The *Halizones* did not see the last of her explosives until she had been to Calcutta. All through one day in Calcutta, she discharged 760 cases of powder an hour, the work being done exclusively by officers and men of the ship. "All feeling thankful that the last of the explosives have gone," the Master recorded when the work was over.

The long journey home was uneventful until the vessel ran into wild weather as she neared England. She also had a visitation from a German aeroplane, but the gunners who had dealt with a submarine (or a whale) also dealt with the aircraft. The plane was flying very low and although it disappeared in the mist, the gunners thought they had scored one or two hits.

The *Clan Ross* was another ship to run into the gale as she came home through the North Atlantic. She had taken a cargo of naval and military stores to the Middle East and had then gone on to India. In all her long voyage, she had suffered only two ineffectual air raids by Italian planes while on her way up the Red Sea to Suez.

Also safely back in Liverpool at the beginning of March, 1941, after a voyage "On His Majesty's Service" to Suez, was the *Clan Cameron*. Only two days before reaching Britain, she had had a grim encounter. It was about 10 a.m. on March 2 that the look-out of the *Cameron* sighted a vessel stopped and not under control. Approaching the ship, Captain H. Andrews, Master of the *Clan Cameron*, realised that she was a Dutch vessel which had been bombed only two hours earlier. He decided to close her to pick up any survivors. As he did so, an R.A.F. plane appeared and helped the British merchantman locate a lifeboat in which were thirty men. Among them was the Second Mate of the Dutch ship. He told Captain Andrews that there was an unexploded bomb on the Dutchman.

At the same time, the aircraft signalled that there was an upturned lifeboat on the starboard side of the ship. Captain Andrews decided to board the Dutchman. A lifeboat was manned and he himself went over to the vessel. Climbing on board, he explored the damaged ship and found the unexploded bomb. He considered ways and means of saving the Dutchman but as he could not dispose of the bomb and native members of her crew refused to return to her to raise steam, he was reluctantly compelled to abandon the bombed vessel. He knew, too, that the British aircraft had reported her position to the naval authorities. Captain Andrews had done his best and it was unfortunate indeed that, after pulling back to his own ship, the heavy swell caused him to slip on the rope ladder and fall about ten feet into the lifeboat, injuring his back. The crew of the Dutch vessel were landed at Liverpool by the *Clan Cameron*.

Chapter Four

The Navy's Admiration

The Merchant Navy, with Allied comrades, night and day, in weather fair or foul, faces not only the ordinary perils of the sea but the sudden assaults of war from beneath the waters or from the sky. Your first task is to bring to port the cargoes vital for us at home or for our armies abroad, and we trust your tenacity and resolve to see this stern task through. We are a seafaring race, and we understand the call of the sea. We account you in these hard days worthy successors in a tradition of steadfast courage and high adventure, and we feel confident that that proud tradition of our island will be upheld to-day wherever the ensign of a British merchantman is flown.

MR. CHURCHILL'S MESSAGE, JULY, 1941

THE GERMANS CONTINUED WHAT MIGHT BE TERMED THE "TIGHT blockade" of the British Isles until March, 1941. Up to that time practically all our losses in the Atlantic were in the eastern half, with a few hundred square miles of approach waters to the north-west of Ireland as the most-favoured hunting-ground of the U-boats.

Although it was not widely recognised at the time, we won the first round of the longest battle of the war when we forced the enemy to hunt further afield. Seven U-boat sinkings in one month helped to shake off Hitler's strangle-hold and prepared the way for new methods of countering the threat to our vital shipping lines of supply.

The battle spread across the North Atlantic and down to the African and South American routes. Little, if any, relief was forthcoming for our merchant shipping. The shortage of escort vessels was still acute and, although Catalinas were beginning to make a useful contribution in covering convoys within a few hundred miles of our shores, there was a very big mid-Atlantic gap which only long-range aircraft could fill.

Whichever way the battle swayed, the Red Ensign ships carried on, and the Germans were perhaps beginning to learn that liberties must not be taken with vessels that had only one gun worth mentioning. The *Clan Colquhoun* helped in this lesson while on passage with an outward convoy on March 8.

An enemy aircraft, coming in confidently, dropped three bombs close to other vessels in the convoy, and then found itself at no great height over the Clan ship. An attempt to scare off opposition by machine-gunning the poop was unsuccessful. The gun's crew of the *Clan Colquhoun* opened fire and, cheered on by those on the bridge who could see the effectiveness of the fire, riddled the fuselage of the enemy plane. The German was last seen heading off at about fifty feet above sea level and apparently unable to regain height.

The *Harmodius*, of the Houston Line, was among the first ships to suffer as the U-boats went further afield. She was torpedoed when in convoy about six hundred miles off Cape Blanco on March 8. It was a grim night, three ships being torpedoed within a space of ten minutes. First the *Tielbank*, about four cables astern of the *Harmodius*, was struck. Five minutes later the *Nordana* was a victim, and then, as Captain R. J. Parry tried to swing his ship so that she would not give the hidden enemy a full-sized target to aim at, the third torpedo struck home. The explosion blew up the port side of the bridge and furniture from some of the officers' cabins was thrown out on to the deck. One of the boats was smashed but the others were got away, with the exception of No. 5 lifeboat which tipped up, flinging nine men into the water. Survivors of the *Harmodius* were picked up by H.M.S. *Faulknor* and landed at Gibraltar some days later.

It was very shortly after this that Captain J. McCrone, Master of the *Clan Maciver*, nearly turned the tables on the U-boats. Outward bound for the Cape, he had his officers on double watches, lookouts on the wings of the bridge and two gunners on duty on the gun-platform. His ship had just started a third leg to the zig-zag that had been going on all day when, between squalls of sleet and rain, one of the lookouts on the gun-platform reported a submarine surfacing 200 yards away on the port quarter. It was 8.45 p.m., wind was at gale force and visibility was only moderate. It was fine work, therefore, to spot a submarine just coming to the surface. And within a few seconds it was clear that the lookout had saved the ship. As soon as his report was received on the bridge, the helm was put hard-a-starboard. The *Clan Maciver* turned just sufficiently to let a torpedo which was fired at her, pass under the starboard quarter not more than five yards from the ship.

Captain McCrone passed the order for "Utmost Speed" as the remainder of the gun's crew closed up. He then discovered for the first time that another submarine was in the vicinity. The *Clan Maciver* continued to take evasive action until, suddenly, at 9.20, the second U-boat surfaced. It was about 300 feet away on a parallel but opposite course. In Captain McCrone's own words: "the temptation was to ram, but the disadvantages of this manœuvre were obvious, so I turned away and opened fire."

The first shell was delayed for a fraction of time and only later did those on the bridge discover the reason. The enemy was so close that, with the gun-sights at zero, the gun would not bear until the *Clan Maciver* rolled slightly towards the target. Spindrift lashed at the eyes of the gunners and heavy seas came over the after deck, but the first shell, fired before the U-boat had completely surfaced, was a "near miss". The submarine was lit up in the gunflash.

The second round was fired with the enemy at a distinct disadvantage. At right angles across the stern of the *Clan Maciver*, he could make no use of his torpedo tubes. The Second Officer, who was in charge of the gun's crew, thought the U-boat had been hit, as its long, dark hull was hidden by a fountain of water. Captain McCrone, whose coolness had been largely responsible for saving his ship in the earlier stages of the encounter, did not agree with this view.

"What it did do," he declared later, "was to cause the enemy to carry out a crash dive—which must have been a record for this manœuvre in the German Navy—and break contact. We never saw him again.

"Full use was made of dense volumes of oil smoke coming from the funnel," he added, "and smoke floats were dropped where we felt they would give us most effective aid. At 2 a.m., what was taken to be dimmed signalling was seen some two miles off abeam. This was brought astern and we made our way from the area with alacrity. By dawn, the weather had deteriorated to a full gale, with poor visibility."

This modest "Captain Courageous" gave credit for the saving of his ship, firstly: "to the excellent lookout of the gunner on watch" and, secondly: "to the sound co-operation of all concerned, both on deck and in the engine-room."

He urged that all members of the gun's crew should be accommodated together with an alarm bell in their quarters. Some of the men had not heard the klaxon horn, which was the signal for "Alert", and he had had to send an apprentice from the bridge to bring them together, "with the consequent loss of a pair of eyes on the bridge when they could ill be spared."

In one valuable night's work, Captain McCrone not only taught the enemy a lesson but learned one himself and passed on the benefit to hundreds more.

This was acknowledged by the Director of the Trade Division of the Admiralty in a subsequent letter in which he said: "The promptness with which the enemy was engaged and the accuracy of the fire clearly indicates the efficiency of the defensive organisation of the ship." He asked that his congratulations might be conveyed to the Master, Officers and members of the crew of the *Clan Maciver*.

Ships arriving in United Kingdom ports in March and April, 1941, had a variety of experiences to report. The *Clan Macarthur* and the *Clan Lamont* both came back after "O.H.M.S." voyages round the Cape and up to Alexandria. The *Macarthur* had twice taken R.A.F. and military personnel and stores to Piræus, and she claimed the distinction of being the first ship to unload 250 lb. and 500 lb. bombs there. Of seventeen nights spent in Alexandria only three had been free of bombing. Two other alarms had been experienced in very different quarters of the globe. On the way to Colombo, where she went after completing her duties in the Mediterranean, she had made ready to fight when challenged by a suspicious vessel which ultimately turned out to be a friendly warship, and, when nearly home, she had fired a couple of satisfying rounds at a U-boat eighty miles south of Iceland.

The *Empire Song*, the *Clan Chattan* and the *Banffshire* arrived home from long voyages within a few days of each other. The *Clan Chattan* had made a fast run on the Colombo-Durban leg of her homeward trip after being warned that a raider was in the area. The convoy in which the *Banffshire* made the voyage from Freetown to this country had twice been attacked by U-boats, five ships being lost. The *Empire Song* had her chief adventure when she was practically in port. Having trouble with her compass, she was being led by a naval tug towards the boom defence when the "in" and "out" control lights were suddenly changed. The tug stopped smartly, having more regard for the lights than for the big ship astern of her. Although the engines of the *Empire Song* were at once rung from "Dead Slow" to "Full Astern", the "bump" could not be avoided and, although no very serious damage was done, the *Empire Song* lost the useful services of the tug.

Bad news came from Piræus in the first week of April. It was that the *Clan Fraser*, one of the ships that had got supplies through from the west to Malta, had been lost after being bombed in port.

None of those in Piræus at the time is likely to forget the end of the *Clan Fraser*. Arriving on April 4, she had started to unload her cargo of military stores. It was on the evening of the 6th that she was struck by three bombs during an air raid on the port. Other bombs landed on the quayside and warehouses at the same time, and the task of fighting the fires in the *Clan Fraser* and getting the wounded ashore was made more difficult because the ship drifted away from the quay.

The bombs landed forward, amidships and aft in the ship. Among five European members of the crew killed were Mr. Hogg (Chief Engineer), Mr. Owen (Fourth Engineer) and Mr. Anderson (Sixth Engineer), who were on the after deck at the time of the bombing. Radio Officer Ollason, Gunner Howard and two Indians, also lost their lives.

One bomb-burst swept everything off the bridge, and Captain Herbert J. Giles was knocked unconscious. "A brick from the warehouse dropped on my head and brought me round again pretty quickly," he said afterwards.

The wounded were got off the burning vessel by dragging

them through the water on a line made fast to an overturned crane by a plucky Indian quartermaster who swam ashore with it. For four hours the *Clan Fraser* blazed fiercely and then, when she was red-hot from the bulwarks to the water-line, she blew up. The explosion, which was tremendous, did great damage in the port and shook buildings twelve and fifteen miles inland. It was a sad end to a fine ship, the only fortunate circumstance being that casualties among her crew were not as heavy as they might have been.

An account of a narrow escape from disaster in another harbour—Gibraltar—was given by the Master of the *Clan Macdonald* when she arrived back in Liverpool in April, 1941. After an adventurous voyage from England, during which cruiser escorts of the convoy had engaged a powerful enemy surface raider, the *Clan Macdonald* had reached Gibraltar on the turn of the year. On the night of January 1, Captain A. MacKinlay, after receiving warning of a gale approaching the port, told the engineers to stand by and ordered all hands to stations. As a prelude to the gale, heavy squalls of wind and rain swept over the shipping towards midnight. When the full force of the gale broke in the early hours of the following morning, one of the ships of the convoy was blown ashore.

Captain MacKinlay had been running his starboard engine dead-slow astern to ease the strain on the after wire. But then there came one of those strange twists which test the ingenuity of the best of sailors. The wind abated, and then suddenly changed in direction and blew harder than ever. At 5 a.m., with the barometer still falling, it was blowing at hurricane force. What they had been fearing in the *Clan Macdonald* happened. The forward moorings carried away from the buoy, and then the after wire went. The ship drifted towards the vessel that had gone ashore earlier.

The naval authorities on shore could give no aid, and they

expected at every minute to see the *Clan Macdonald* crash into another ship in the full anchorage. But Captain MacKinlay had acted promptly. Almost as soon as the moorings parted, he gave the order to let go the port anchor and then began to swing the ship to windward by an expert manipulation of his powerful engines. Having got the *Clan Macdonald* round in the teeth of the gale, he steamed clear and let go the other anchor. But he found the anchors would not hold in the face of the enormous wind force.

Using his engines continually, Captain MacKinlay fought for five hours to save his ship, and then, because the anchors continued to drag, he calmly signalled to the shore for permission to leave harbour. This was granted, but the tough Master of the *Clan Macdonald* still had one more difficult round to fight.

When he gave the order to heave up the anchors, it was found that they had fouled buoy moorings. For an hour and a half, in a biting wind blowing at gale force, members of his crew worked to clear them. At 3 p.m., more than twenty-four hours after he had taken his first precautions against the gale, Captain MacKinlay steered his big vessel out through the breakwater and anchored safely in twenty-five fathoms.

Next day, when the weather moderated, Captain MacKinlay was requested to go ashore. He received the unusual honour, for a Merchant Navy Master, of personal congratulations from the Vice-Admiral Commanding, North Atlantic, who stated in a subsequent report: "It is considered that in avoiding a collision or grounding under the prevailing weather conditions and in the very congested harbour, the Master displayed fine seamanship."

The *Clan Macdonald* proceeded through the Mediterranean with a cargo of munitions bound for the Piræus. She had the distinction, not always a pleasant one in these waters, of being

Commodore's ship. She survived repeated attacks by high-level and dive-bombers and was shelled as she passed through the narrows. Nevertheless, she arrived safely and discharged her valuable cargo. Going by way of the Suez Canal, the *Clan Macdonald* went as far as Brisbane before returning to this country.

"On the homeward run, nothing of importance to report," said Captain MacKinlay, "until our arrival at anchorage, when a bomber dived down at four o'clock in the morning and dropped two bombs about twenty feet from the ship's side—and flew off before we could fire our guns." So the record of one more outstanding voyage ended on a note of: "And that's that."

One of the constant problems of these far-ranging ships was fuel. Many of them could use either coal or oil. Sometimes coal bunkered in far distant ports was of poor quality, and Masters, warned of the presence of a raider, made quick changes to oil in order to increase their speed. But oil, too, had its drawbacks. The *Clan Macquarrie*, for instance, found herself making heavy black smoke which "covered the horizon for twenty miles" when using oil on an outward run. The engineers did everything in their power to improve matters, because it was known that six U-boats were within a radius of 200 miles and the convoy with which the *Clan Macquarrie* had sailed had been dispersed. Still the tell-tale smoke drifted away behind the vessel and everybody was thankful when a succession of severe south-westerly gales came to hamper the movements of the submarines. While still on the way to Cape Town, a change was made to coal, and it was then possible to keep the smoke, which had been such a serious menace, under control.

Four vessels of the Clan fleet had sailed in a convoy of between fifty and sixty ships which left Freetown on March 12,

1941. They were the *Clan Ogilvy*, the *Clan Macnab*, the *Clan Macilwraith* and the *Clan Macwhirter*. They had come together from various parts of the world for the final run home. Two of them were fated never to reach Britain, but it was not until weeks later that their varied stories could be pieced together.

Collision accounted for the *Clan Macnab* when the convoy was only five days out. In the evening of the 17th, the convoy was attacked by one or more U-boats and, after a ship had been torpedoed, the Commodore ordered several sharp emergency turns. At 10 p.m. the *Clan Macnab* had to alter course to avoid collision with another ship but, less than an hour later, a ship appeared out of the darkness only three cables ahead of the *Macnab*. The Master, Captain P. G. de Gruchy, ordered the helm to be put hard-a-port but the other vessel struck the Clan ship just abaft the bridge. Although it was obvious that serious damage had been done to the shell plating, the *Clan Macnab* continued with the convoy until the early afternoon of the next day when it was decided that she should break away and make for the Cape Verde Islands. After three hours, however, she sank and, although the boats were got away, three subsequently submerged in the rough sea and fourteen members of the crew lost their lives.

The *Clan Ogilvy* was torpedoed and sunk three days later. She had sailed from Liverpool just five months before and had had a narrow escape when German four-engined bombers attacked the outward-bound convoy. On the homeward run from Calcutta, she had arrived at Freetown on March 1, to find that a convoy had just sailed.

After waiting eleven days, she set off with the big convoy of March 12, which included the battleship *Malaya*. When the U-boat attack developed on the night of March 20, the warship was the first to suffer. About an hour later, the *Clan Ogilvy* was struck by a torpedo which blew off the propeller and exploded the magazine, killing the gun's crew and a number of Indian seamen. It was a mortal blow to the *Ogilvy* and in less than four minutes after the explosion the after deck was awash.

Captain E. Gough gave the order "Abandon Ship," but owing to the number of men killed only three boats could be got away. "All living souls were off the *Ogilvy* when I myself slipped down the lifeline into No. 1 boat," Captain Gough later reported. "As we pulled away, the bulwarks on the after deck were below water and a fierce fire was raging in the poop space."

The last to be seen of the *Ogilvy* was when the emergency oil lamps, which had helped the crew to get away, were doused as the ship made her final plunge. From that moment, a further long-drawn-out ordeal began for those in the boats.

A vivid description of what happened to No. 1 boat was given by Captain Gough—but not before he had experienced a second torpedoing, which will be referred to in due course. "As daylight approached on March 21," he wrote, "mast and sail were hoisted and a survey made in the hope of locating the Chief Officer's boat. Several rafts and some wreckage were sighted and then a lifeboat under sail, which I thought was the First Officer's boat. But on making contact we found it was the sole surviving boat of the S.S. *Benwyvis*. There were forty-three men in the boat, and on a raft, which was being towed, were nine more, including Captain Smalls. The nine men from the raft were transferred to my boat and ten men from the lifeboat of the *Benwyvis* were put into the *Ogilvy's* boat, of which Second Officer Freestone was in charge.

"At about 10 a.m., after consultation with Captain Smalls, it was decided to make for Cape Verde Islands, proceeding under separate sail during daylight and making a tow during the hours of darkness. This procedure was adhered to for ten days, when it was obvious that we had missed the islands. On

"After hits with eight inch shells from the "Cornwall" the raider blew up and broke in two"

the morning of March 31, owing to shortage of water, it was decided by all boats to proceed at utmost speed on a course of East (True) in order to cross the trade routes to South America. It was agreed that the boat fortunate enough to be rescued should give the whereabouts of the other boats."

The bald, courageous account of Captain Gough continued: "At noon on April 1, I sighted a neutral steamer heading north-east. Distress signals were made but, although we were only about three miles off, our signals were unanswered. At about 6.30 p.m. the same day, a light was sighted on the port bow, heading in what appeared to be a south-westerly direction. I stood on my course of East and the steamer's lights became clearer. We closed to within 200 yards under full sail, inner and outer jib, mainsail and jigger, before making our presence known. Red lights were then burned and the crew of the life-boat shouted, while torchlight was flashed on the sails. The vessel immediately responded by giving a prolonged blast on the siren. By 7.30 p.m., all hands were rescued and were on board the S.S. *Cabo Villano*, of Seville, under the command of Captain Don Luis de Arsuaga y Sagardui."

Captain Gough described how messages were sent out asking all vessels to keep a good lookout for the other boats. The *Cabo Villano* stood-by until daybreak but then, with no lifeboats in sight, proceeded on her voyage. No praise was too high for the Master and crew of the *Cabo Villano*, who provided dry clothes and did everything in their power for the British sailors.

And this is what happened in No. 1 boat of the *Ogilvy* during the twelve days' sailing, according to Captain Gough's account: "The weather was fair, the trade wind blowing fresh during the afternoons and early mornings. A hand log was constructed from the hank of boat lacing which was carried and an extra jib and jigger sail were made from the boat cover. Our speed was found to vary from two to four knots. Water was rationed from the first day, the ration being about one tablespoonful at 6 a.m. and another at 6 p.m. If the day was extra warm, I allowed one water dipper between six men at noon. On the second day out, we opened a large tin of corned beef for the evening meal. Half was eaten then and half the next morning. This was the only canned beef that was eaten during the twelve days because it made the men so thirsty. Our diet consisted of a small amount of condensed milk—sometimes mixed with the portion of water and sometimes spread out on a biscuit. After three or four days, one did not feel like eating and a biscuit lasted two days. The malted milk tablets were distributed at 3.30 p.m. each day—one to each man—and these were found to be very sustaining."

Captain Gough also described a strange encounter—almost certainly with a U-boat—which took place three days after they were torpedoed. "On the night of Sunday, March 23, all boats were hove-to, heading north-west, when, at about 11 p.m., a dark object suddenly appeared on the starboard quarter at a distance of 200 yards," he wrote. "This object proved to be a submarine 'breathing' on the surface. When Captain Smalls burned a red flare, the submarine crash dived. A minute or so afterwards we saw a green flashing light about one mile away—apparently another submarine. We immediately altered course to South and never saw them again."

The physical ordeal of Captain Gough and his men, hardly referred to in the narrative, was indicated in three sentences: "When we were rescued by the *Cabo Villano* and landed on her deck, it was found that our legs were more or less useless. I had to hold on to the bulwark rail to prevent myself from falling down. It was at least seven days before I could walk the length of the forward deck and back without wanting to sit down."

Unhappily, it was an ordeal that was to be repeated for the Captain and three members of his crew, well within two months. They sailed from Santos for England on May 6 in the S.S. *Rodney Star*. Ten days later this ship was torpedoed, and Captain Gough again found himself occupying a small open boat some hundreds of miles from land.

As the four lifeboats got clear of the *Rodney Star*, the attacking U-boat put two more "tin fish" into the ship. And Captain Gough, who might well have recorded feelings of despondency, gave this lively description of the half-an-hour that followed: "As we drew away from the *Rodney Star* she appeared as if nothing had happened and this apparently annoyed the submarine commander, because the U-boat surfaced and promptly commenced to shell the ship. When we were about three miles away from the *Rodney Star*, sail was lowered in three of the lifeboats so that we could see the effect of the gunnery—which appeared to be rather poor. Our sails were only down for a couple of minutes when, behold, a shell plopped right into the middle of the four boats, and only about 150 feet away. Needless to say, sail was again hoisted! It was 10.10 a.m. before the ship sank, after three torpedoes and about seventy rounds of ammunition."

Following three days of doldrum weather—light winds and torrential rain—Captain Gough was again among those rescued at sea, this time by the S.S. *Batna*, which took him and his shipmates to Takoradi.

Final chapter for Captain Gough was a successful run home in the S.S. *Abosso*, although this in itself would have been eventful enough for most people. Submarines dogged the convoy, and the Master of the *Clan Ogilvy* had the satisfaction of seeing two despatched by naval escort ships. Then a vessel laden with palm kernels was hit and flames shot 200 feet into the air. A second victim, a ship with a cargo of manganese ore, sank in seconds rather than minutes, but the attacker was detected and sunk. Attack and counter-attack continued, and three more vessels in the convoy were lost, but the *Abosso* got through. This last cool comment of Captain Gough should not be allowed to pass: "After an all-night sitting with the U-boats, we were very grateful when tea was passed round in the lounge."

It will be remembered that, on the morning after the *Clan Ogilvy* had been torpedoed, search was made by Captain Gough for the boat under the command of Mr. H. C. Carter, his First Officer. Contact was not made, but the First Officer's boat was also heading for Cape Verde Islands. A system of lookouts was instituted in the boat and supplies were carefully rationed, but on March 27 it was reluctantly decided that the islands had been missed, and course was set for the mainland. The men in this boat also had the galling experience of sighting a big ship which failed to see them or their signals. Late in the afternoon of April 4, land was sighted, but another night had to be spent in the boat. Next morning, with the land about twelve miles away, there was a flat calm and the crew of the boat were too weak to row. A light wind came after midday, and by 4.30 p.m. the Chief Officer had negotiated some dangerous breakers and the boat had grounded two miles off shore. Natives came out to aid the exhausted sailors as they stumbled through the water towards the coast of Portuguese Guinea. That night, while the men slept in the mud huts of a native village, a runner got through to Portuguese officials at Suzana. The following day, the survivors of the *Clan Ogilvy* were taken to Suzana by canoe, and then, by various stages, they moved on to Bissao. On the very last part of their journey, disaster overtook twelve Indian members of the crew. A lorry in which they were travelling overturned, three of the men being seriously injured.

"Red lights were burned and
  the crew of the lifeboat shouted."

At Bissao, all the survivors were well treated, especially by the British Vice-Consul, Mr. Adams, and Miss Fricker, a missionary. More than a month later, Mr. Carter led his little band back to England by way of Bathurst and Freetown.

When the final count was made, it was found that twenty-six members of the crew of the *Clan Ogilvy* had lost their lives.

The other two Clan ships that had set out with the convoy from Freetown, the *Macilwraith* and the *Macwhirter*, arrived in England at the end of April, but not before they had made a double crossing of the Atlantic. On the evening of March 21, the Commodore had ordered the convoy to scatter, and both vessels had made their way safely to Halifax where they subsequently joined an eastbound convoy.

Four Clan ships, if one includes the *Empire Song* which was under the same management, were in another convoy which sailed into the Mediterranean under strong naval escort in May. The convoy was subject to heavy air attack, and on the night of the 8th, when about forty-five miles west of Pantellaria, the *Empire Song* was badly damaged and her No. 1 hold was set on fire by a mine or mines. A plucky attempt was made to save the ship, which was carrying military stores and ammunition. Efforts to put out the fire were unsuccessful and internal explosions shook the *Empire Song* as she steamed on. The temperature in No. 1 hold went up to 110 degrees, and then Captain William Jennings gave the order to abandon ship. But he, with the Chief and Second Officers, the Chief, Third and Fifth Engineers, the Chief Radio Officer and Apprentice Taylor, remained on board. The explosions became more frequent and the fire was obviously spreading when they eventually left the *Empire Song* at 2.15 a.m. on May 9.

Two hours later, a party of volunteers, including the Chief Engineer and the Second Officer, set off from the destroyer which had picked them up, with the intention of re-boarding the *Empire Song*. When their whaler was thirty yards away from the ship, she blew up. The boat went to pieces and the explosion caused considerable damage to the destroyer but all the volunteers were saved.

The other three ships, the *Clans Lamont*, *Chattan* and *Campbell*, got through in the face of numerous air and under-water attacks. The *Clan Campbell* had to overcome engine trouble, and a signal made to her from the battle-cruiser *Repulse* expressed the admiration of the Navy for the pluck and perseverance of their Merchant Navy brothers. It was: "On arrival at Gibraltar I shall report to the Flag Officer in Charge the great work you and your engine-room staff have carried out in overcoming your difficulties. I feel you have done great service to the country and I shall take care to see that it is known at home."

While ships in many seas faced great hazards, those at home in port were not free from danger. In Liverpool, where German bombs were raining down, the *Clan Macinnes* could prepare this grim log:

Sunday, May 4: Heavy explosion at 2 a.m. caused buckling of midship deck and outside shell. No. 1 beams and hatches blown into lower hold. Starboard list on ship; several fires dealt with during the night. Ship making water in forward holds.

Monday, May 5: Various fires dealt with during the night.

Tuesday, May 6: Shed doors blown on to side of poop by near miss. Several bombs close to vessel and fires dealt with. 5 a.m., unexploded bomb found in No. 5 hold. Evacuation of ship ordered by police. Bomb dealt with by disposal squad—crew returned.

Wednesday, May 7: Salvage pumps at work continuously in forward holds. 1 a.m., ship shaken by heavy explosion. Shell plating opened on port side. Fires dealt with. . . .

In comparison with this, several ships arrived home about this time, or a little later, with nothing more to report than slight engine trouble, or, as in the case of the *Clan Murray*, five minutes on the mud in the Thames estuary. It was at the sailing of this ship that one of those things beyond explanation, which brought to mind the ugly word "sabotage", happened. The engines suddenly stopped and the vessel was compelled to haul out of the convoy and anchor to prevent drifting into a mined area off Harwich. On examination, a bolt was found in the bottom of the cylinder.

Captain A. Campbell brought the *Clan Macaulay* safely back from an Admiralty charter trip to Malta, and to a modest two-page report on the voyage, attached this handsome tribute from the C.-in-C., Admiral Sir Andrew Cunningham: "I have much appreciated the work done by you, your officers and crew, on the station, under difficult circumstances. Our task is made much easier by such resolute handling. I hope you have good luck in all your future voyages."

If the *Lanarkshire*, which had twice accomplished the 1,800 miles round trip between Alexandria and Malta during her ten months away, received official congratulations, her Master, Captain E. Coulthart, was even more modest. To a similarly brief report he merely attached a table of sailings which, in bare figures, disclosed that he had sailed more than 40,000 miles. But one fact he did mention was clearly indicative of the feelings of the Navy towards his ship. "Ship's personnel has worked well together during some very trying times," he wrote, "and we are happy to state that H.M.S. *Fermoy* presented us with their ship's crest in Malta when we were about to leave the port for the last time. I have taken the liberty of installing this on the saloon bulkhead."

The "trying times" referred to by Captain Coulthart included no less than forty-two air raids experienced at sea, in Malta and in Alexandria. And the *Lanarkshire* escaped damage!

Towards the end of July, 1941, first accounts reached this country of the loss of the *Clan Buchanan* and the tragic fate which subsequently overtook her Master and many of her crew. While on her way from Durban to Colombo, she had been intercepted by a German surface raider, after being sighted by the raider's aircraft.

Captain D. Davenport Jones had stood up to some concentrated shelling and had not surrendered until his ship was helpless, debris which was blown into the engine-room having stopped the engines. While under fire, all secret codes and mail in the *Clan Buchanan* were destroyed and the Second Radio Officer got a message away asking for help and then smashed his set to prevent the Germans using it for an "All Clear" message.

Although a number of hits were scored on the *Clan Buchanan*, none of her crew was killed and they were transferred to the raider. Their ship sank shortly afterwards. It was the account of Chief Officer S. S. Davidson as to what happened subsequently, that reached England in July.

"We were ten days aboard the raider," he wrote, "in a cell at port side No. 2 'tween deck, and during this time we were well treated, but the food was poor. Our cell held twenty-four, and all our twenty-five Europeans were there, but three days after joining the raider, the Steward, Carpenter and four gunners were transferred to another cell among European sailors and lascars from the *Empire Light*. During our daily two to three hours exercise on deck, we met the Officers and Engineers from the *Empire Light*, who told us they had been

THE NAVY'S ADMIRATION

captured three days previous to ourselves. We all kept in excellent health and spirits during our sojourn on the raider and her Commander expressed to Captain Jones his satisfaction and pleasure on our behaviour and conduct. On May 8 (a.m.), Captain Jones was informed that in the event of an air or surface raid, prisoners were to be removed to an alleyway on deck to give them a chance of escape if the vessel was hit. This they unfortunately did not do.

"There was great activity on the raider during the day," Mr. Davidson's story continued, "and at 4 p.m. we could hear the guns being cleared for action. Immediately, they opened fire and the noise was terrific—a gun right overhead shaking our cell every time it fired. This lasted about ten minutes. Then there was a terrific blast, sweeping everyone in our cell off their feet and hurling them into a corner. When I picked myself up, I found I was opposite to the door, which was open. (Later I was informed that it had been opened just prior to the blast.) We all marched up a flight of stairs to the shelter deck and immediately went to the ship's side (side being open to allow concealed guns to fire) and looked out. I saw half the ship under water and the rest going quickly. I shouted to Captain Jones, who was near me, that she was sinking fast and to jump quickly. He waved his hand, and those around jumped with me as the ship heeled over to starboard and started to sink quickly by the stern. On reaching the water, I turned round to look at the ship and found her with her bows right in the air. She was gone in five seconds.

"Captain Jones was last seen with his foot on the ship's side, smoking his pipe. I think he and the others waited too long to jump and were thrown off their feet when the ship heeled to starboard, and went down with the ship."

The raider had been sunk by the British cruiser *Cornwall*, in the execution of her duty. They picked up as many survivors as they could, and their satisfaction at disposing of a menace in the Indian Ocean must have been sadly affected when they learned of the loss of life among British seamen. After hits with 8-inch shells from the *Cornwall*, the raider blew up and broke in two. Only eight Europeans and five Indians of the crew of more than 100 taken from the *Clan Buchanan* were picked up.

The *Perthshire*, which had had a rough time in Malta in the spring, arrived in Liverpool from Australia in August, 1941, and Captain C. D. Worthington, her Master, described how, after leaving Brisbane, mock attacks by fighters and bombers were carried out on the ship "to familiarise us with the real thing".

He did not say whether he informed the air and naval authorities that, in the course of the same voyage, his crew had experienced bombing up and down the Mediterranean and had spent twenty-seven days in Malta, during which their ship was hit by several bombs and set on fire. Through this ordeal, the behaviour of both European and Indian members of the crew was excellent.

On her way to Cape Town in August, the *Clan Macpherson* became a "mercy ship" to twenty-seven officers and men of the torpedoed S.S. *Macon*. The men were suffering severely from exposure after ten days in an open boat, and some of them had to be hauled on board with ropes. The officers of the Clan ship shared their quarters with the officers of the *Macon*, and all the rescued men were made comfortable. Twelve were treated in the ship's hospital, as advised by the Medical Guide, and the "doctoring" was so satisfactory that, although some of the *Macon's* men had been unconscious or delirious immediately after being rescued, all the patients were well by the time the *Clan Macpherson* arrived in Cape Town.

Sailing from the Tail of the Bank at the end of June, 1941, the *Clan Forbes* rounded the Cape and made fast alongside at Alexandria on August 23. Discharge of cargo continued night and day, and was completed on September 3—an appropriate anniversary.

Chapter Five

From Southend to the Barrier Reef

As the importance of our being strong at sea was ever very great, so in our present circumstances it has grown to be much greater because, as formerly our force of shipping contributed greatly to our trade and safety, so now it is become indispensably necessary to our very being.

HALIFAX, 1694

TWO YEARS OF THE WAR AT SEA HAD GONE BY, BUT THERE WERE no signs in September, 1941 of the struggle becoming any less severe. More than 200,000 tons of Allied shipping fell victim to U-boats in that month alone. But the dogged spirit of the Merchant Navy remained unshaken. The Royal Navy, doing its utmost to offer protection to the carriers of supplies, sank seven U-boats in the same month.

Among the vessels arriving in the Mersey in September were two ships of the Houston Line, the *Harmonides* and the *Halizones*. Both vessels had "come of age" in the previous twelve months, and a ship at twenty-one, unlike a human being, has no long vista of years ahead of her. But the two "H's", both of a little more than 5,000 tons gross, seemed in the prime of life as they came home again after six months at sea.

The voyage of the *Harmonides*, in particular, may be taken as a fair example of the hazards that had to be faced at this time. She had sailed from the Royal Albert Dock, London, in the early daylight of March 8, a full ship, with 3,500 tons of cargo, 1,883 tons of bunkers, Nos. 1, 2 and 4 ballast tanks full, and 360 tons of fresh water in No. 3 and after peak tanks. Compasses were adjusted after proceeding down river, and then she anchored to await convoy.

The Germans knew all about those anchorages by "the gate". It was also a common sight to men in ships, but nothing could have been more inspiring to hard-hit Londoners, if it had been possible to let them see it, than a view of the convoys assembling. It would, no doubt, have surprised our seamen if they could have seen the admiration on the faces of Commando men on one occasion, when they found themselves in a large congregation of ships in the Thames estuary.

It was an odd chance that took the Commando men there, and they had plenty on hand to think about, but they looked at the grey ships and received fresh inspiration. If plans had not been altered at the last moment, the Merchant Navy would unconsciously have inspired men on the very eve of desperate battle. The Commando ship had come through the Straits of Dover covered by a slow convoy, and she was accepting the same type of cover when she anchored not far from Southend. When darkness fell, she was due to slip out, and, on the other side of the Channel, the skilled fighting men she carried were going ashore to give a strong force of Germans the surprise of their lives. A last minute intelligence report meant a complete change of plan. The Commando men steamed away north to their base and I travelled in a leisurely train from Southend to London—with the never-to-be-forgotten savage roar of disappointment with which the special service troops had greeted the news that the raid was off, ringing in my ears.

To return to the voyage of the *Harmonides*—she sailed from Southend in a nine-knot convoy of sixteen ships, bound for Methil. Soon after the pilot was dropped in the Mid Barrow Deep Channel, the convoy ran into dense fog and twice had to anchor. Early on the morning of March 10, as the convoy steamed on, Captain H. Evans, Master of the *Harmonides*, realised that an air and surface attack was being made on ships ahead. Vessels became scattered, and it was more than twelve hours before the convoy reformed.

Arriving at Methil, there was the usual conference attended by all Masters, and then the *Harmonides* sailed in a six-knot convoy of thirty-five ships. When off May Island, the convoy was joined by an equal number of ships from the Tyne, bound coastwise and overseas. Speed was not increased until the overseas section of the convoy separated at Skerryvore to proceed to Oban.

At another conference there, Captain Evans was informed that the Admiralty insisted that a Lewis gun's crew of two men should be signed on Articles as deck hands at one shilling per month. The *Harmonides* left Oban with sixteen other vessels, and the main convoy was made up with ships coming from the Mersey and Clyde. It was an eight-and-half-knot convoy of forty vessels, bound for all parts of the world, with a "seeing off" escort of ten destroyers and corvettes and a specially-equipped rescue ship.

Only one quiet day was spent at sea and then, at daybreak on the 19th, an enemy aircraft flew in from astern. The gunners of the *Harmonides* got off a few rounds, but the aircraft, flying at only a few hundred feet, passed over another column of the convoy and dropped its bombs. Only one scored a hit but, as the ship blazed, Captain Evans remembered that he had been told by her Master that he had a few hundred tons of explosives on board. What Captain Evans, and others who watched anxiously, feared, very quickly happened. Several small explosions took place as the rescue ship approached the burning vessel and then, with a violence that shook every other vessel in the convoy, the stricken ship blew up. Everything was hidden in a great column of smoke encircled by the splashes of falling debris. When the smoke cleared, it was seen that the forward half of the ship had been blown away, while the other half had been swept clean of all deck erections. To the hiss of escaping steam, the half a ship disappeared—only thirteen minutes after the bomb had struck home. Miraculously, there were eleven survivors.

That night the convoy suffered another air attack but no ship was hit, and it is hardly surprising that when another plane appeared at daybreak the next morning, it had a warm reception, although those trained in the art of aircraft recognition declared it to be one of our own.

On this day, March 20, the convoy dispersed, and the *Harmonides*, zig-zagging south, picked up messages asking that a lookout should be kept for the boats of the *Clan Ogilvy*, the *Benwyvis* and another ship. She arrived safely at Cape Town on April 17, and, with a big convoy in, waited three days at anchor before a berth could be found for her. Then came calls at Simonstown, Mossel Bay, Port Elizabeth, East London and Durban before proceeding to India.

At Calcutta, the *Harmonides* loaded 2,500 tons of pig iron and, a little later, at Cocanada, large quantities of tobacco and ground nuts were put into the ship. Remaining space was filled at Colombo with tea, rubber and plumbago. Monsoon weather was encountered on the way to Cape Town, where 100 tons of jam was added to the cargo. The *Harmonides* made her way home by crossing to Halifax and joining an east-bound convoy of forty-nine ships, the only excitement being provided by a British man-o'-war which came "out of the blue" when the merchantman was six days on her way from the Cape. The *Harmonides*, not certain as to the identity of the warship bearing down on her, sent out a distress signal which was quickly cancelled once visual signals had been exchanged.

Covering the same waters as the *Harmonides*, the *Halizones* was machine-gunned in the North Sea, and went through another convoy-versus-aircraft episode on her first day out of Methil. Reporting an uneventful passage to Freetown, Captain Jack E. Townrow mentioned that wireless messages picked up on the way indicated that they were having some "very near misses" as far as contact with U-boats was concerned.

The long passage to Australia was safely completed by the *Halizones*. Fully loaded, she left Townsville on July 20 and, arriving off the Arlington Reef the next day, disembarked the Torres Straits pilot and commenced the homeward passage outside the Great Barrier Reef, reaching the open sea two days later.

Sailing in the tracks of the great explorers, Captain Townrow made this observation: "Although I found no difficulty in navigating the above course, I would not recommend it to Masters during the rainy season, when observations may not be obtainable or compass errors checked. The reefs and islands are low lying and currents uncertain. I would suggest that the Queensland Government Pilotage Service be approached with a view to their arranging for the Torres pilot to be disembarked off Port Curtis (Gladstone). If this could be arranged, a course could be set to pass clear of Lady Elliot Island, after which a vessel could come to little harm, no matter what the weather conditions."

Five days before arriving at Balboa, the *Halizones* received information that she was within fifty miles of an enemy surface raider. The report was received in the late afternoon and the subsequent laconic comment of the Master was: "happily we had all the dark hours before us."

Captain Townrow, it may be said, had an almost Drake-like touch on occasions. Hurrying on from Port Royal, Jamaica, to Norfolk, Virginia, and thence to Halifax, Nova Scotia, to catch the fast convoy home, he recorded with satisfaction that he received his instructions from the Naval Control on the day following the main conference of Masters and then "returned on board and had a nice hot bath." Having passed through a dense belt of fog soon after heading out into the Atlantic, the weather came in cold and clear and the Master of the *Halizones*, preparing his report, wrote: "As I type we are enjoying cold but bright sunshine and the sight of sixty fine ships, in nine columns abreast, keeping perfect station, is a sight to please the eye." And a few days later, after a stormy but safe passage, he wrote: "We anchored off the Queen's dock this afternoon at a little before four o'clock, all feeling very thankful to find Liverpool still standing, and to have won at least one more round of the Battle of the Atlantic."

There was little "swapping of yarns" even among Masters during the war. They had not much opportunity of getting together and when they did, it was probably in the shadow of a poster with a slogan such as "Walls have Ears", which they knew all too well to be the truth. Just occasionally one met a Master who, in the proper company, unburdened his soul. Such a one was the brave Norwegian sailor I sat listening to well into the early hours of a winter's morning in Londonderry. He had sailed an open boat over 400 miles of the Atlantic for the second time in his life. The first occasion had been twenty-odd years earlier when he was little more than a boy. A natural sailor from the peace-loving northern country, he told me his story and gave his verdict: "The Germans are barbarians and should always be treated as such by all men who live by the sea."

No doubt, if he had talked at all, Captain C. C. Parfitt, Master of the M.V. *Clan Macdougall*, would have said much the same when he stepped ashore in Glasgow early in October,

1941. His ship had been lost very shortly after sailing from St. Vincent on the night of May 31. No submarine was sighted but two torpedoes struck home and it was a wonder that only two men—one of them the Seventh Engineer—lost their lives. Arriving in Freetown, Captain Parfitt had found more than 1,000 officers and men waiting there under similar circumstances to himself. Sailing in the S.S. *Silver Belle*, he had been torpedoed again and had been among the volunteers to go back to the ship when she was found to be still afloat. The final vivid picture in the mind of the British Master as he walked through the busy streets of Glasgow must have been of the surviving remnants of the convoy of thirteen ships that had started home from Freetown. Only four ships got through.

But Captain Parfitt spoke only of the exemplary behaviour of the crew of the *Macdougall*. "My Lascars were worth three of some other crews," he said with pride.

The convoy system, and congestion in ports that were taking more traffic than they had ever known before, caused many delays. Masters were the first to draw attention to this, although, knowing the difficulties, they seldom registered a complaint. The *Clan Mactavish* reported being delayed at Cape Town, having to wait for a convoy at Aden, and spending five days after discharge of her cargo at Port Said. Of another port where delay occurred, Captain R. J. W. Bennet said: "There were so many vessels for repair that the Port was not fit to undertake so much work and convoys coming in had preference even over warships."

The formidable total of lost days that could be built up for even a single ship was best illustrated, perhaps, by the faithfully set down time-table of the *Clan Macneil*. Having started from this country with an ill-fated convoy that lost twelve ships in twenty-four hours, the *Clan Macneil* suffered these delays: Freetown, 5 hours; Cape Town, 5 hours; Durban,

5 days 3½ hours at anchor; Durban (second visit), 9 days 5½ hours awaiting orders; Aden, 2 days 1 hour; Suez, 3 days; Port Said, 1 day; Alexandria, 1 day 3½ hours; Port Said (second time), 15½ hours; Suez (second time), 1 day 18 hours; Calcutta, 11 days 7½ hours for de-gaussing; Durban (third visit), 2 days 6½ hours waiting for bunkers; Cape Town (second time), 1 day 2 hours waiting for bunkers; Trinidad, 2 days 4 hours for bunkers and 1 day 14 hours for engine-room repairs; Halifax, awaiting convoy, 5 days. Nearly seven weeks lost in a wartime voyage of less than eight months!

There were other things beside delays to contend with. The convoy system, which gave more and more protection to merchantmen as the Navy's surface and air strength increased, was a constant strain on Masters and Watch Officers. Commodores and Senior Officers of Escort Groups were, on the whole, considerate and patient but there were times when the Merchant Navy officers felt a little aggrieved.

The Master of one Clan ship was told before leaving Halifax that the Commodore of the convoy would take steps, by use of his radio, to muster any ships that became detached. The convoy, it was said, would leave harbour at six knots, and that speed would be retained until the whole convoy mustered.

The Clan vessel was the last to leave harbour and, to the Master's surprise, the convoy was out of sight. By working up to eleven-and-a-half knots, he caught up with a tanker but, in the darkness, lost his sole companion. The Master had been given a rendezvous for noon the next day and, making for that point, he duly sighted the lost convoy. The Clan ship took up her station in deteriorating weather with thin rain and moderate to poor visibility. Her stay with the convoy was short. Although there were no alterations of course during the next night, the convoy had disappeared again when daylight came. Again in the company of one other vessel, the Clan ship steamed on for five days. Then, quite alone once more, she picked up a radio message which told her that her last companion had been torpedoed thirty or forty miles away. The Clan ship had to keep on her lonely way to England, where she arrived safely, twenty-four hours ahead of the main portion of the convoy, which came in after its proper formation had been broken up by foul weather and other causes.

In fairness to courageous and skilled sailors—many of them veterans of the sea—who volunteered to serve as Commodores of Convoys, and not only shared the dangers but made the same great sacrifices as those with whom they sailed, it must be emphasised that experiences of this nature were very much the exception.

Major and minor anxieties were the lot of those in command of ships through these trying years, and it was not always possible to distinguish between one category and another. On a voyage of the *Clan Macgillivray* which lasted for more than six months in 1941, Captain B. Vernon Browne was faced with at least two minor mysteries that might easily have turned into major disasters. The first ocurred when he was a week out from the Mersey and at the very moment the convoy was due to disperse. Fitted in the after part of the ship was a powerful arc-lamp for use in fog. At 1 a.m., when all ships were slipping away quietly on their different courses, this lamp was suddenly switched on. "Its glare," in the words of Captain Vernon Browne, "must have been visible at a distance of twenty miles." The closest inquiries failed to reveal who was responsible for this strange and extremely dangerous happening.

The other incident occurred weeks later when the *Macgillivray* was passing down the Mozambique Channel on the passage between Madras and Durban. Again it was a "light" mystery, but this time the light came from another ship—if ship it was. The *Macgillivray* was called up in morse on a brilliant lamp. This was all against procedure and Captain Vernon Browne immediately brought the light on the quarter and answered the challenge, but there was no response. A warning signal was sent out on the *Macgillivray's* radio and answers were received from shore stations as far apart as Aden, Mauritius and Cape Town. After some forty minutes of W/T "alert", the British ship returned to her former course.

Compass trouble, an unsuccessful search for boats after a distress signal had been received, a mail bag which had had the attentions of a thief, a severe burn to one of the engineers, some slight disciplinary troubles and a normal share of engine disorders were among the minor anxieties of the Master of the *Clan Macgillivray* on the same voyage.

In what he described as "a very safe berth practically in the middle of the convoy", Captain R. Douglas of the *Clan Macquarrie*, prepared the report on his voyage, as they sailed the last leg from Halifax to Liverpool during the latter part of October and the beginning of November, 1941. It was a safe berth only by comparison with those of the "wing" ships who, for five consecutive nights as the convoy headed for the northern channel, suffered attacks from U-boats which, with a boldness accounted for possibly by their strength, operated on the surface in bright moonlight.

Captain Douglas knew what was going on, although, as he said himself, he could not get a very good view of the incidents. But the recording of another incident that had happened five months earlier must have compensated Captain Douglas for his obscured position on the run home. It had come about on the day the outward convoy broke up. For an uneventful week up to 4 a.m. on May 20, the ships had been in company. They then separated, and the *Clan Macquarrie*, veteran of two wars, set course for the Cape. At

11 a.m., the wireless operator reported to Captain Douglas that two ships had been torpedoed about thirty miles to the south. The Captain immediately took the unpalatable course that Merchant Navy Masters had to follow throughout the war. He turned away from the scene of danger and did not swing back to a southerly course again until he had covered sixty miles. It should never be forgotten that, facing almost continuous danger as they did, the men who manned our merchant ships in war hardly ever experienced the uplifting thrill of going in to the attack. Their task called for a calm courage, patience and, if necessary, fortitude in the face of suffering, with no glory beyond the eternal glory of the Red Ensign under which they served.

Proceeding on a zig-zag course at a speed of thirteen knots, Captain Douglas first suspected that a U-boat was in close proximity when, at about noon, he saw what looked like a tide rip travelling slowly northward about six cables ahead. He stopped zig-zagging and went straight for the head of the tell-tale ripple. Five minutes later, there was a terrific impact immediately under the foremast of his ship. The bows appeared to rise and for ten seconds the whole ship shivered under the force of whatever was under the hull. Then there were two more severe bumps, one under the deep tank amidships and the other under the mainmast. Captain Douglas concluded that he had landed practically on top of a U-boat. For ten seconds, the *Clan Macquarrie* rode over the submarine and forced her down. Then the buoyancy of the under-water craft forced her up and she bumped twice more on the bottom of the merchantman.

After those satisfying bumps, Captain Douglas looked astern but nothing appeared above the surface of the water. It is unlikely that anything from that particular submarine ever did. After the coal had been worked out of the deep tank and before the *Clan Macquarrie* arrived in Cape Town, it was found that six frames on the port side and five on the starboard had parted from the ship's side. This damage was quickly repaired in Cape Town and the stout old *Macquarrie* went on to complete her voyage according to schedule.

On December 1, 1941, the ex-French ship *Desirade* arrived in the Mersy under the command of Captain J. D. Matthews of the Clan Line. Almost exactly a year earlier, he had sailed from this country in command of the *Clan Cumming*—and a book could be written about the adventures that befell the Master and crew in that twelve months.

A start was made on these adventures before the *Clan Cumming* linked up with the main convoy, the Clyde section being unsuccessfully attacked by a U-boat on December 22, 1940. Three days later, on Christmas morning, the main convoy was attacked by a surface raider, and shells fell between the aircraft-carrier *Argus* and the *Clan Cumming*. Visibility was poor and those in the *Clan Cumming* could only see the orange flashes that accompanied the rumble of heavy guns. Two ships received direct hits, but it was reported that, although the raider had escaped, her supply ship had been sunk. Then the order was given for the convoy to scatter. The Clan ship, alone in a heavy gale, was overtaken by engine trouble, but eventually made her way into Gibraltar. The gale continued to blow, and one ship, with 400 troops on board, went ashore. The troops were divided among the *Clan Cumming* and three other vessels remaining in the convoy, which set sail eastward on January 6, 1941.

Three days later, the first wave of enemy aircraft appeared. It was a high-level attack by the Italians who, meeting strong opposition from the escort, were satisfied with several "near misses". Next day, the German dive-bombers arrived, and it was in the course of their persistent attacks, in which most ships had narrow escapes, that the aircraft-carrier *Illustrious* was badly hit and set on fire. How she survived is now a matter of history. "In this scrap" (to quote Captain Matthews), "we had only four slight casualties—three soldiers and Apprentice Robb. The Apprentice got a piece of shrapnel in his arm while manning the high-angle gun, but he stuck it out until the end of the action."

More Stukas attacked, but the *Clan Cumming* arrived safely in Piræus and discharged her troops and valuable cargo. She sailed again with a strong escort, but, on January 18, was torpedoed forward. Although under-water plates could be seen projecting at right angles to the ship's side, the *Cumming* struggled back into Piræus without having suffered a single casualty. But there her luck—if luck it could be considered—ceased. It is true that over a period of two months in dry dock, she escaped a direct hit, although she was often the main target. But the *Cumming* was still in Piræus when the Germans opened their attack on Greece, and her crew witnessed the destruction of their sister ship, the *Clan Fraser*, and the devastation of the port as a result.

"Why, while there yet appeared to be time, no steps were taken to tow the *Fraser* out of harbour, will remain a mystery," Captain Matthews wrote, in a particularly graphic account of that dreadful night. "It must have been known by the Authorities that there were some hundreds of tons of high explosives on board her, but beyond a small tug which played a hose over her No. 3 hatch from alongside, nothing seemed to be done. Commander Knox, Lloyds' surveyor, and I watched her burning from my lower bridge till 2 a.m., and, since she was red hot fore and aft just above the waterline, we concluded—wrongly—that if there were still high explosives on board, they would have exploded before then. Commander Knox went ashore in his row boat and I lay down half-dressed. I was nearly asleep when—the whole world seemed to burst asunder! The *Cumming* went over until she seemed to be on her beam ends, and then rolled heavily for some time. All the woodwork in the rooms crashed down and then came the rain of molten metal falling, which had to be seen to be believed. Among other things we had a full plate, 23 ft. by 3 ft., wrapped round our main top. About half the *Fraser's* windlass crashed through our No. 4 hatch and set fire to timber, etc. Later, a section of structure was found nearly three-quarters of a mile away. It weighed twelve and a half tons. About thirty feet of her 80-ton derrick was found in a park. Before the blast, I had counted fourteen deep-water ships, four hospital ships, two cruisers (*Ajax* and *Coventry*) and numerous coasting craft and barges. In a very few minutes every one of them was on fire, including ourselves. We got our fire hoses going and had the worst of our fires out when an officer of the *City of Roubaix*, which was alongside to port, hailed me with: 'Our water system has failed; we are badly on fire and fifty tons of T.N.T. in No. 2 hatch will go up any time. Send a boat for us and abandon your own ship while you have time.' The Greek ship to starboard, full of cotton, was blazing fiercely, so it was apparent that I would have to abandon, at least temporarily. This was done in good order, a boat going to the *Roubaix*. When she blew up, I was watching from the shore, and when the smoke and debris had cleared I could see the *Cumming* still intact but on fire fore and amidship. The military had stopped all traffic, so it was not until later in the morning that five of the crew and myself could get on board to put the fires out. The *Devis* and *Cumming* were the only two deep-water ships saved from this catastrophe, which even the pen of Dante could not adequately describe."

Even after this experience, the trials of the crew of the *Clan*

Cumming were far from over. Fierce dive-bombing attacks were made by the Germans with the British ship as No. 1 target, but still she escaped a direct hit. Eventually, on April 14, Captain Matthews got his Seaworthy Certificate. The *Cumming* survived one more heavy air attack that night, during which she claimed to have shot down a bomber, and then she sailed. The escort that had been promised failed to appear, and at 11.20 p.m., when the *Cumming* was four and three-quarter miles north of the charted minefield, a gun was fired and she received a warning in morse: "Danger from mines, you should alter route to north." Captain Matthews headed his ship to the north but two other warnings followed. Almost simultaneously with the last: "You are in immediate danger," there was a heavy explosion and the ship began to settle fast by the stern. The order was given to abandon, and, in Captain Matthews' words: "Poor old ship—at 3.28 a.m. she was out of sight."

Picked up by the Greek destroyer *Queen Olga*, Captain Matthews and his men suffered more air attacks before being put ashore. The Master got through to Athens and reported to the Admiral heading our Naval Mission. His next contact with the Admiral was in Crete, when they were both trying to buy a shirt!

When the Germans broke through in Greece, Captain Matthews and his men "hiked" their way to the Corinth canal and then down to Nauplia, getting what food they could on the way. For two days they lived in a cornfield—"luxury compared with the stony hillside"—and then, with nothing more than they stood up in, they were taken in H.M.S. *Phoebe* to Suda Bay, Crete. Again they slept in the fields until they could be evacuated to Alexandria. It was two months later, during the long and broken journey home round the Cape, that Captain Matthews received orders to take over the command of the French ship he eventually brought into Liverpool.

The *Clan Macinnes*, coming home in convoy from her last port of call, Gibraltar, had a memorable Christmas. For six days and nights in succession, the convoy was attacked by bombers and submarines. Three enemy planes were shot down, but a light aircraft-carrier with the convoy was sunk by a torpedo which was intended for the *Macinnes*. Captain R. Parry saw the torpedo coming and put his helm hard-a-port. The torpedo passed a few feet ahead of his ship, but, running into the middle of the convoy, struck the carrier.

The *Clan Macinnes* got through safely and Captain Parry was able to report how, on the outward voyage, his gunners had shot down a German bomber. It was a remarkable instance of the alertness of gunners in a merchant ship. When the aeroplane was first sighted ahead of the convoy, the Commodore hoisted the signal: "Friendly aircraft." One of the escort ships disagreed and opened fire. Within a minute or two it was proved that the escort was right and the Commodore wrong. Flying so low that it appeared to hop over the ship ahead of the *Macinnes*—dropping a bomb on her as it did so—the aircraft went straight for the Clan ship. When the range was only 1,500 yards, Captain Parry ordered all guns to open fire. Still the plane came on, flying no more than thirty feet above the sea. Suddenly, when it was right over the ship, the starboard wing was seen to crumple and the plane crashed into the sea. "The wing was cut off by the Hispano gunner," Captain Parry afterwards decided. "There were no survivors; they were all killed before the plane crashed, I think.

"From then on," the Master added, "we had a fairly quiet time with only an occasional submarine scare."

Apart from taking a useful hand in the fighting, the merchant vessels were ready to assist the Navy in other ways. The *Clan Chattan*, for instance, towed one of the convoy escort ships for twenty-seven hours when she ran out of fuel.

On the turn of the year, four of the Clans, *Ross*, *Skene*, *Macbrayne* and *Macaulay* returned from long voyages. The *Macaulay* had been seriously on fire at sea on the way home from Australia but her Master, Captain A. Campbell, stated that his officers and engineers behaved superbly and the outbreak was overcome after a stiff struggle. The *Clan Ross* had been to Bombay and the Malabar coast, and the *Skene* and *Macbrayne* to Calcutta, Chittagong and Madras. Back in home waters, the *Macbrayne* prepared for a night attack by enemy aircraft. Bombers could be heard circling overhead above the clouds, but the first the sailors saw of the Germans was when one bomber, after a burst of fire from our night fighters, came spiralling down in flames.

The *Clan Macpherson* successfully ran the submarine gauntlet both outward and inward, and Captain Charles O'Byrne noted that for part of the homeward run across the Atlantic, destroyers of the United States Navy were the escort. He arrived back in Britain at the end of January, 1942, and, as the presence of the American warships indicated, events of vast significance had occurred since he sailed in the preceding summer.

The Master of the *Clan Macindoe* (Captain A. J. Hogg), also safely home in the new year, recorded that, in accordance with Admiralty instructions, he had employed one of the naval gunners in his ship to aid the anti-sabotage watch while in port. For this duty, the gunner received extra pay at the rate of four shillings for each watch.

The *Clan Colquhoun* came in in February, 1942, after a voyage that had lasted all but a year. In a one-page "Incidents Report" Captain A. G. Storkey told of an attack by a Junkers

88 when his ship was three days out from this country. The Third Officer, Mr. Macintosh, had opened a well-directed fire with the port Hotchkiss, and, with the plane passing astern at a height of only 150 feet, two Lancashire Fusiliers, manning the Lewis guns, had pumped a steady fire into the fuselage. The bullets had been seen cutting holes along the side of the plane. On the way home from Australia, there had been an encounter with the Dutch cruiser *Tromp*, when the *Clan Colquhoun*, unabashed by the warship's guns, had refused to stop because the Dutch vessel had not answered with proper recognition signals. Apart from that, there was apparently little to say about a year's voyaging beyond the fact that "the Yorkshire coal supplied at Birkenhead caused unusually heavy smoke and most violent abuse from the convoy Commodore."

In February, too, the *Clan Macdonald* returned, and Captain A. MacKinlay was able to tell the story of a remarkable voyage through the Mediterranean. His way home from Gibraltar, oddly enough, had included calls at Australian ports. The excitement had started ten days after leaving Gourock with a special convoy protected by a large force of warships. An air-sea battle developed in which fourteen enemy planes were seen to be shot down. The *Clan Macdonald* had narrowly missed being torpedoed. On September 28 she was safely in Malta with her full cargo of munitions.

On October 16, she began one of the most spectacular runs undertaken by a merchantman during the war. Four children were among eleven passengers put on board by the naval authorities, and then the *Clan Macdonald* slipped out alone and made her best speed to the westward. Having passed through the dangerous narrows by night, Captain MacKinlay, on instructions, hoisted the French flag and continued boldly on his way in broad daylight. It was not long, however, before an aircraft appeared and began to circle the "French" merchantman. In the ship they thought it was a French aircraft but, at midday, three more aircraft came and joined in the circus. Uneasy suspicions, which must have been growing on both sides, were confirmed when one of the planes flew in low and across the bows of the *Macdonald*. It was low enough, in Captain MacKinlay's estimation, to be able to see the ship's name. The Master, looking anxiously skywards, had no difficulty in seeing the Italian white cross tail markings on the three-engined machine. Still, the British bluff was not called, and the aeroplane that had flown over the ship headed off towards Sardinia, while the others continued their circular shadowing.

It was more than three hours later when another trio of Italian planes appeared. Having circled the lone vessel, one of them came in with the sun behind him and dropped a torpedo. It was a near thing for the *Macdonald* but, the torpedo having missed, Captain MacKinlay ordered the French colours to be hauled down and the Red Ensign to be run up in their place. At the same time the gunners in the merchantman opened fire. A second plane got into the attacking position and dropped a torpedo. Only a quick change of course saved the *Macdonald*, the torpedo running parallel with the starboard side and only five feet from the ship. The aircraft followed up with a mine, which was also wide, and some machine-gunning, but, opposed by fire from the Clan vessel, his bullets did not reach the ship.

When the third plane took up the attack, the *Macdonald's* gunners had their eye in, and hits were scored with the port oerlikon. The machine staggered, lost height and then rose, and that was the signal for the Italians to break off the engagement. It was too much to hope that this was the end of the trouble for a single ship running the gauntlet of the Mediterranean. Two hours later, the watchful gunners in the *Macdonald* saw a Cant torpedo-bomber approaching from the northward. As this aircraft prepared to attack, the Clan ship turned into the sun and the oerlikon gunners opened up. Hits were scored at once and two puffs of black smoke came from the aircraft. At the same time it banked and, apparently badly damaged, flew off without attempting to launch its torpedoes.

Next day, one plane flew over at a respectful height, circled the Red Ensign ship, and then departed without making an attack. The *Clan Macdonald* sailed into Gibraltar on the morning of October 19 and had the signal honour of a visit from Admiral Sir James Somerville. His congratulations were reinforced by a letter from the Board of Admiralty.

In addition to fighting his way through, Captain MacKinlay had had the knowledge that if his ship was stopped by a man-o'-war and a boarding party put off to take her as a prize, he was, in his own words: "to take the necessary measures to prevent same being carried out."

Chapter Six

The Enemy in the East

That which was and is the strength of this Nation
—the Shipping.

OLIVER CROMWELL, 1654

THE PERIOD ROUGHLY COVERED BY THE SPRING AND SUMMER
of 1942 opened on a good note. A large force of U-boats had
been operating off the east coast of the North American
continent and in the Caribbean following the entry of the
United States into the war in December, 1941. Many ships
had been sunk in this area but there had been a compensating
improvement in the position on the North Atlantic convoy
routes. In March, 1942, more than 400 ships in nineteen
convoys came in through our north-western approaches
without a single casualty due to enemy action.

But before we consider this period more generally, we must
go back six months earlier and pick up the threads of the
Clan Forbes' story, which we broke as she completed her
discharge of cargo in Alexandria on the second anniversary
of the outbreak of war.

We can follow her rather strange fortunes for a year—and
leave her at the end, much further away from home than at
the beginning. From Alexandria, the *Forbes* went to Port
Said where she received her discharge from Government
charter. The Master, Captain H. Cater, made preparations
for sailing south on normal business, but, next day, found

"Bombs fell all around the 'Ferguson'
and one perfect 'straddle' landed two
on either side of her without doing
any real damage."

that his release had been cancelled and that he was to go to Suez. Another twenty-four hours, and he learned that his ship was to be fitted out to carry 400 troops on a very secret expedition.

One more instance of the Merchant Navy's ability to take everything in its stride was presented by Captain Cater's almost casual comment on this rather sudden and startling move. "Armed with this information," he wrote, "I endeavoured to find out something more concrete from the various authorities I thought might be concerned with the business, but drew a blank." The Senior Transport Officer, who went to see the Admiral, was only slightly more successful. The troops, he was able to tell Captain Cater, were Royal Marines of the Mobile Naval Base Defence Organisation. The Master was to victual them for fourteen days.

Now this was a matter of real concern to Captain Cater because provisions were scarce and expensive and he had not the necessary personnel to do the catering. Help came from the Colonel commanding the force. Realising the difficulties of the Merchant Navy Master, he detailed Marines to act as cooks and bakers and was "very successful in collecting the cooking utensils necessary for the voyage". Shortage of labour and supplies made it impossible for the contractors to complete the re-fitting of the ship, and the Marines themselves loaded hundreds of tons of their own equipment in order that it should be on board for the very definite sailing date. It included mechanical transport, travelling cranes, excavators, landing craft and big gun battery equipment.

All this went on against time, and not without attention by the enemy. Although the *Clan Forbes* was not near any important military objective, air raids came almost nightly, and Captain Cater decided it was perfectly apparent "that if the local authorities had no knowledge of the vessel's employment, the enemy certainly had some information".

The *Forbes* sailed to time on a pitch-dark night, the decks still littered fore and aft with everything imaginable from Sawyer stoves to motor landing craft. Fitting out was far from complete, there being no water service other than the galley or pantry taps, no bakehouse, no lights in officers' quarters or on the troop decks and only one galley stove situated on the foredeck. In the day-time, when temperatures were in the high nineties, there was no awning to provide cover for the troops. Officers were accommodated in boxlike "rooms" erected on each side of No. 3 hatch. Four officers' shared each room of six feet by six feet, light and ventilation coming from a hole cut in the back.

But the Royal Marines, remembering their proud motto, *Per Mare Per Terram*, did not complain. On the contrary, the tradesmen among them got to work and rapidly improved matters. Escorted by the cruiser *Cornwall* and in company with H.M.S. *Glenroy*, who had more of the M.N.B.D.O. troops on board, the Clan ship headed for "Port T". Presently it became known that this was Addu Atoll in the Indian Ocean, and that a "port" was the last thing that was likely to be found there.

Arriving at the atoll, a suitable landing place was chosen, and the troops went ashore in the landing craft and began to establish an encampment. Roads had to be made and then the work of preparing gun emplacements began. The coral reef around the islands of the atoll provided the boats with plenty of trouble and the *Clan Forbes* became a Depot-cum-Repair ship. It transpired that her troops were originally intended to proceed to the Nicobar Islands but, by the time they had completed their share of the work on the atoll, the Japanese had progressed far enough to cause this plan to be altered.

The troops found their "deserted island" an unhealthy place, and when the *Clan Forbes* eventually left for Colombo and Calcutta to load more stores and equipment, she took many sick men with her. Her return to "Port T" was like "bringing relief to a beleaguered garrison", to use Captain Cater's words. The men on the island were short of stores and nearly all their boats needed attention.

When the *Forbes* again left the atoll she had a part to play in the fortifying of Diego Garcia, but she had not seen the last of Addu. From time to time she called there until the hopeful news came that, the Ministry of War Transport being insistent, the big merchantman was to be released from her semi-Service duties. A final trip from Bombay with a "parcel" for Addu was planned. Arriving in Bombay, Captain Cater discovered that the "parcel" consisted of 1,000 Indian artisan Ratings. The Ratings were embarked, but when the *Forbes* finally sailed from Bombay seven weeks later—after being docked and undocked five times—she went to Colombo without the Indians. Her next voyage was to Seychelles with more Marines. After another visit to Addu, there came further reports that the ship would shortly be released, but September, 1942, found the *Clan Forbes* once again on her way to the atoll, and her special service was to extend for another three months.

.   .   .   .   .

The splendid support rendered to Malta by Clan ships during those dark days was carried on by the *Clan Ferguson* almost where the *Clan Macdonald* left off. Surviving bomb and torpedo attacks, the Ferguson arrived at the island about the time the *Macdonald* was leaving on her unescorted run to the west. She had sailed from the Clyde with 245 troops and a full cargo of war material. The *Ferguson*, also without escort, followed in the wake of the *Macdonald* a week later, but, after suffering several attacks by Italian torpedo bombers, she was ordered back to Malta.

For a month the *Ferguson* remained in harbour and then, with three other ships, she had the unenviable task of sailing as a decoy. It was late in the year and the Italian Navy preferred to remain snugly in port, so the *Ferguson* returned to Malta and, continuing to load scrap, spent Christmas there. On the evening of Boxing Day she left with a small convoy bound for Alexandria. The convoy had frequent visitations from enemy bombers and the bombs fell close enough to inflict above-water damage on the Clan ship. The *Ferguson* got through in time for Captain Lofthouse and his men to spend the New Year in Egypt. Then the ship was loaded again with a full cargo of general war material, explosives and foodstuffs for Malta. In addition she took on 1,000 tons of fuel oil and 270 tons of coal.

With 175 troops as passengers, she sailed again for Malta on January 16. By submarine and air attacks, the enemy made every effort to stop the supplies going through. One merchant ship and a destroyer of the escort were sunk, but the *Clan Ferguson* again brought relief to the garrison and people of Malta on January 19. After discharging her cargo, she spent four days in dock having her bottom cleaned, which must have seemed like a final gesture of defiance to the frequently raiding aircraft from the north.

She left Malta on February 13, to run the gauntlet for the fourth time in less than four months. Despite the date, her luck held, and Captain Lofthouse himself was prepared to use the word "miraculous" when he reached Port Said. For forty-eight hours after leaving Malta there were continuous air attacks. Bombs fell all around the *Ferguson*, and one practically perfect "straddle" landed two on either side of her without doing

"A large
flying boat
with German
markings
circled over
the rafts"

any real damage. Captain Lofthouse's only comment on the great strain of such service was in the report: "I have nothing but praise for the whole personnel on board, native crew included, for the admirable way in which all have assisted and stood up to the severe, nerve-racking experience of the last few months."

The long road home for the *Clan Ferguson*, with a variety of cargoes, was by way of Bombay, Cape Town, New York and Halifax. It was June 18, 1942, when Captain Lofthouse wrote from Loch Long anchorage: "We arrived at five o'clock this morning and are now busy discharging explosives."

On the last day of March, 1942, an attack with an unpleasant form of novelty about it was made on the *Clan Macinnes* during passage from Durban to Trincomalee. What happened is dramatically told in this summary prepared by the Master, Captain A. Lynch, at the time.

1400. Sighted a two-masted Dhow, hull down four points on port bow. Course altered to bring it abeam and Z.Z. discontinued. The Dhow was heading approximately southeast.

1430. Masthead lookout reported an object dead ahead. Nothing of this could be seen from the bridge, nor by another lookout who was sent aloft. Z.Z. was resumed. The Dhow was now hull up and making good way through the water as a bow wave was distinctly seen although the sails were flapping. It was heavily rigged, with a high stern, the upper part of which was painted white. There were two leg-of-mutton sails and also an oblong topsail on the foremast and one jib on a boom.

1515. The ship ported three points on the leg of a Z.Z.

1516. A submarine, with conning tower above water, was seen about three-quarters of a mile away, lying two points abaft the starboard beam. Immediately after we sighted it, a torpedo was fired from the forward starboard tube. We were porting to bring the submarine astern. When it lay about two points on the port quarter, the port tube was fired. This was about five or six seconds after the first shot. The tracks of the torpedoes could be distinctly seen and followed. They were narrow, white, and ran perfectly straight. By using helm and watching their runs, I manoeuvred so that one ran along the starboard side about fifty yards away and practically parallel with the ship, while the other ran under the stern and exploded at the end of its run. I watched the end of the run of the one on the starboard side and it curved to the right—away from the ship. The gun's crew had been closed up and a periscope was seen in the wake aft. This was fired at and the shot evidently went over—a near miss. Nothing more was seen until 1540. Then what was apparently a periscope feather was sighted about one to two points forward of starboard beam. This was put astern and nothing more was seen. The weather at the time was light airs, force 0 to 1, smooth sea, swell nil and excellent visibility. From time of sighting the Dhow until the last was seen of it on the starboard quarter, was three hours, and *Clan Macinnes* was steaming twelve knots.

Later, Captain Lynch supplemented this crisp summary with a few more details. Soldiers and naval ratings closed up most expeditiously and the gun-laying of T. Cavanagh was of a very high order, he said. The Indian members of the crew were quite calm.

"After the shot was fired," said the Master, "my boy came and asked me: '*Chaa mangta, Sahib?*' (Do you want tea, sir?). I never appreciated tea so much, for by this time the taste in my mouth was extremely salty and at the same time very dry!"

In these waters a month later, the *Clan Ross* was torpedoed without warning. A second torpedo followed the first and the ship sank very quickly. From the bridge, Captain G. McColl saw the second torpedo heading for his ship but nothing could be done to avoid it as all way was off the vessel. A boat which he stepped into from the deck was washed back on to the sinking ship. Before those in the boat could scramble clear, the vessel went down under them. Captain McColl was taken down some distance and then "suddenly shot up through the water to land about thirty yards away". The forecastle head of the *Clan Ross* was just disappearing.

The enemy submarine surfaced and steamed round the wreckage, but made no attempt to aid the crew, several of whom were still in the water. The Master himself was clinging to a raft. Eleven Indians were missing and the remainder of the crew—seventy-five officers and men—were divided among the only two boats that remained seaworthy after the explosions. Course was set for the coast of India. Survivors in one boat were picked up by a Norwegian steamer and, after sailing for six days, the men in the Master's boat were taken on board a native vessel when only fifty miles from land.

Captain McColl did not enlarge on his experiences but his report contained this significant paragraph: "I should like to recommend that a lock be attached to the water tank, or the tank shipped aft where we could watch it."

Back in Britain, several Clan and Scottish Shire ships were completing long voyages, coming in in rapid succession towards the end of April and at the beginning of May, 1942. The *Clan Macarthur* had been to Australia and New Zealand and had had a twenty days' voyage across the Pacific which was described by the Master with the one word, "uneventful". Having landed his anti-aircraft gun and its crew in Jamaica on the outward run, Captain Herbert J. Giles was quite rightly not pleased when he found that he was expected to make the homeward run across the Atlantic four months later without a gun. "There was a full moon and we would have had no possible chance of survival had we been attacked from the air," was his comment—after making the voyage with nothing more than four automatic rifles.

The *Perthshire* arrived after calls at various Indian and Australian ports. The most interesting event in seven months' sailing, apparently, was the attractive way the Australians, working from punts, scraped a considerable harvest of coral growth and grass off the hull.

The *Buteshire* (Captain Coultas), home with a full cargo, reported that more than 600 tons of explosives which she had taken out to Trincomalee, were not required when she arrived at that port. After a two days' wait, during which two aircraft were discharged and various signals were made, the explosives were carried on to Colombo.

Another Shire, the *Berwickshire* (Captain Arthur R. Cossar), brought home, among other things, accounts of a slight collision with an Australian corvette on the other side of the world, and the sinking of a U-boat on this. As Commodore's ship in the fast section of a convoy homeward bound from Freetown, word came direct to the *Berwickshire* from the Senior Officer of the Escort that a Liberator had successfully bombed a submarine twelve miles astern of the convoy. They were then four days' sailing from home and the S.O. added: "We were most lucky on Friday night as the U-boat was on our tail all night, and would have collected others to make a combined attack. I think it is quite probable that he would have attacked on Friday night, but underestimated our speed. I gave the Liberator full marks for coming out so far in bad weather."

The *Clan Macneil* returned a few days later—on May 5—

having experienced spells of very heavy weather, during one of which a gunner was lost overboard.

The only ship of the Clan fleets lost in May, 1942, was the *Clan Skene* which was torpedoed while on passage from Cape Town to North America. The ship had crossed the Equator when, in the dark hours of the morning of May 10, two torpedoes crashed into her starboard side within twenty seconds of each other. The first was disastrous, causing a great explosion in the boiler room and killing all the Lascars who were on watch. The Third Engineer, Mr. McGillivray, who was in the engine-room, was badly scalded and had a miraculous escape from death as the water rose to bunker-deck height. He was saved by being swirled into the overboard discharge valve recess.

Before Captain E. Gough gave the order to "Abandon Ship," the plates could be heard splitting and the *Skene* was sagging amidships. In the boats, with the American coast 350 miles away, Engineer McGillivray was treated for his burns and shock. The wrecking of the wireless cabin in the explosions prevented any distress signal being sent until eight hours later, when the lifeboat wireless set was rigged. For twenty-seven hours, with the rest of the men in good health and spirits, the scalded Engineer stood up to the agony of exposure. By then, the two boats had covered no less than seventy-four miles—but they still had a long way to go before reaching land. Fortunately, soon after 1 p.m. on May 11, the United States destroyer *McKean* appeared over the horizon and the survivors were quickly taken on board. The British sailors were given a wonderful reception and, as the destroyer raced for port, everything possible was done for Engineer McGillivray.

Captain Gough declared that no praise was too high for Lieut.-Commander Sweeney, in command of the *McKean*, and later he was equally impressed with the sympathetic treatment extended to his men ashore. McGillivray was rushed to hospital as soon as the destroyer arrived in San Juan. The crew of the *Skene* were taken to various hotels and before they went on by sea to Norfolk, Virginia, every man was presented with a complete change of clothing by the American Red Cross.

More than a month elapsed before another ship that had given good service in the war—and the war before—the *Clan Macquarrie*, fell victim to a U-boat. She was torpedoed when over 600 miles from Freetown. Four boats got safely away, but one was damaged and had to be abandoned when the Master, Captain R. Douglas, went back to take off the Chief Engineer. Two hours after the torpedoing, the U-boat surfaced and fired a number of shells into the *Macquarrie* which had obstinately remained afloat, although the 4-inch and 12-pounder guns on the poop had been awash within a few minutes of the under-water explosion. For more than two hours, the crew of the *Macquarrie* sat in their boats and watched their old ship withstand the German shells. Then she slid beneath the waters, the U-boat disappeared and they stoutheartedly set course for land.

In a convoy of fifty-seven ships which made a safe passage from Freetown to this country towards the end of June, were the *Clan Murdoch* and the *Clan Macfayden*. Both ships had been away for more than six months and both had seen something of the war in the East at close quarters.

Captain Booth, of the *Murdoch*, had this story to tell: "At Mombasa, we loaded 1,200 tons of bombs for Rangoon and 1,000 tons of soda for Calcutta. Sailing on February 3, we had a good run until off the Little Basses, when we were attacked by a submarine. I was able to get the helm over, and the torpedo passed between our counter and log line, only thirty feet away. We were successful in evading 'It' during the night, and arrived at Rangoon on the 19th, where nobody knew anything about us. I take this opportunity of stating how well the native crew behaved, especially the engine-room ratings, who stayed below and steamed all out. At Rangoon, we got only 300 tons discharged, when we were ordered alongside to evacuate 1,000 R.A.F. personnel, with all their stores and equipment. Sailing on the 21st, we called at Akyab, where we loaded four smashed planes, 100 tons of spare parts and 250 ratings. Leaving there on the 24th, we arrived at Calcutta jetties on the 26th and commenced discharging. On March 1, I had word to stop all work and return to Akyab. We arrived on the 4th and discharged 900 tons of bombs and took on board 1,000 evacuees and 2,400 tons of rice."

Several ports were visited and on April 3, the *Murdoch* arrived in Colombo. Captain Booth's account continued: "We had to wait until the cruisers *Dorsetshire* and *Cornwall* were oiled. They left on Saturday night. At 7 a.m. on Easter Sunday, we had an 'Alert'. Presently, we counted about forty planes in the sky and somebody said: 'They have a lot of Hurricanes here.' Then we discovered our mistake. We had a heavy 'doing', which lasted for one hour and forty minutes. We had no casualties but there were three near misses forward. We were very lucky, considering the damage done in the harbour. The barrage put up by the ships kept the dive-bombers up, and we had the satisfaction of pumping lead into one of them. . . ."

The *Macfayden*, after sixteen days in Trincomalee trying to get her cargo discharged, went to Colombo early in March. She spent a month in the harbour, which at that time usually had about fifty ships in it. On March 29, Captain Hinton Browne received orders to quit the port. He left the next day, and although that was four days before the *Murdoch* arrived, he was able to say subsequently: "Our exit from the port was not unconnected with the raid on Colombo a few days later."

The *Clan Alpine*, which arrived in Hull late in June, 1942, was another ship that had found herself fulfilling an unusual role in Eastern waters. Her Master, Captain Charles W. Banbury, had been faced with the urgent request that he should evacuate 600 European women from Batavia to Australia. He convinced the naval authorities that this was a practical impossibility but, a few hours later, had instructions to stop the discharge of cargo and prepare to take on board 1,000 evacuees for Ceylon and India. Captain Banbury received these instructions in a town ten miles away from his ship and he was told that he would be expected to take on stores and water for a passage of about a fortnight and sail in less than five hours' time!

A signal was made to the Chief Officer to prepare the ship for sea, the Chief Steward rushed off to get what stores he could, and the *Clan Alpine* sailed in a little over six hours from the time the order was given. Her amazing human cargo was made up of 851 Indians, 31 Ceylonese, 35 Jews, 35 Chinese, 19 Eurasians and 6 Europeans. Of the total, 767 were men and the rest women and children. There were no spare cabins in the ship, but members of the crew gave up their accommodation to women and children. Still, the majority of the passengers had to camp on the lower bridge and in various parts of the vessel. Fires had to be lit on deck to prepare food for them. Captain Banbury found himself presiding over a modern Tower of Babel, but committees, representative of the different races on board, were formed, and a doctor who was in the *Alpine* reported that the passengers were in good health. After 156 of the evacuees had been landed at Colombo, the British merchantman sailed on to Tuticorin where the rest were put ashore, including one extra—a baby that had been born to an Indian woman the previous night.

Addu Atoll

"Troops went ashore in landing craft."

"During ten trying and overcrowded days the spirit of the ship's company remained excellent," Captain Banbury was able to report.

In Karachi, in June, 1942, a strong protest was registered by the Master of the *Clan Macdonald*, Captain C. C. Parfitt, on an unusual matter. He had sailed from England with "special type" bombs stowed in Nos. 3, 4 and 5 insulated holds. Neither he nor his officers knew that the bombs contained phosgene gas. But, on the way, there was a leakage of gas, and Captain Parfitt pointed out in his protest to the District Sea Transport Officer that his ship was one of the latest freezing vessels afloat and the gas could have been kept at any temperature required if he had been notified before sailing. He raised the question of damage caused to the insulation or brine pipes by the deadly gas. A Lloyds' Surveyor, after inspecting the ship, issued the necessary Certificate to keep her in the dry and perishable cargo carrying class.

In August, 1942, the Mediterranean once again held the stage with what came to be known as the "Ohio Convoy". The *Clan Ferguson*, whose other notable runs to Malta have already been described, was one of the fourteen merchant ships that went in convoy with the tanker *Ohio*—and it was her last voyage. After passing Gibraltar, the convoy had only a few hours of quiet sailing before the enemy opened a massive attack. The aircraft-carrier *Eagle* was one of the first ships to sink. Other vessels were hit as wave after wave of bombers came over, but the *Clan Ferguson* escaped until just after 9 p.m. on the 12th. She was then struck by a torpedo dropped by an aircraft, and at once took a heavy list and began to settle by the stern. Worse still, a tremendous sheet of flame had gone up from the engine-room skylight when the explosion took place and the after end of the ship was soon blazing furiously.

Captain Arthur Cossar realised almost at once that his fine

ship would have to be abandoned. Some of the boats were on fire, but, fortunately, a new type of raft had been put into the *Clan Ferguson* before she sailed from the Clyde. Those of the crew who managed to scramble on to these rafts, paddled frantically with their steel helmets to get away from the sea of flame which soon surrounded the doomed vessel. Each raft-load of men believed that they, and they alone, were all that remained alive of the crew of the *Ferguson*. But when dawn came it was found that sixty-four of the crew, including Captain Cossar, had got clear on four rafts. Many stories could be told of that night of horror, lit by the yellow glow of burning ships and the oil-strewn sea, but one will indicate the heroism of the British sailors who saw it through. An eighteen-year-old boy, Midshipman Allson, was among the survivors from the *Ferguson*. He had only been at sea ten days when he found himself swimming for his life. He managed to reach a small raft. Even then, he had little concern for himself, but pushed the raft ahead as he swam, and picked up his exhausted shipmates. Coming upon a larger raft, he transferred the men to it and continued to use the smaller one himself in order to make further rescue sorties throughout the night.

In daylight, Zembra Island was still in sight, but, knowing it to be hostile territory, no attempt was made to reach it. At about midday, a submarine on the surface came towards the survivors. Their disappointment can be imagined when they saw that it was flying the Italian flag. The submarine stopped about thirty feet from the rafts, but after the men of the *Clan Ferguson* had told the Commanding Officer that they were British, the submarine moved off again. About two hours later, a large flying-boat with German markings circled over the rafts and then alighted on the sea. A gun was trained on the survivors and they were called upon to surrender. Half the survivors were then transferred to the flying-boat, the other half being told that they would be picked up in two hours' time. The crew of the flying boat showed every consideration to the British seamen who were injured.

The plane did return but apparently dared not alight because of bad visibility. Sometime later, a Red Cross aeroplane picked up all the men from two of the rafts and flew away to the northward. When only a mile from Cape Bon, Captain Cossar's raft fell into the hands of an Italian motor torpedo-boat. The men on the fourth raft, who were led by Second Officer A. H. Black, managed to get ashore on the mainland. They were interned by the "Vichy" authorities and had a number of strange adventures before getting into Algeria.

It was later in the month of August that a full account reached England of the sinking of the *Clan Campbell*, which had taken place in the Eastern Mediterranean on March 23. The ship was struck by an aerial torpedo during bad weather. Captain J. F. Vooght was among about thirty men who lost their lives. When he headed out on the voyage from which he was destined not to return, the Master of the *Clan Campbell* had no illusions about the dangers of his task. Six weeks earlier his ship had received a direct hit while on the same hazardous route to Malta. The *Clan Campbell* had been forced to put in to Tobruk and had then returned to Alexandria. She had discharged her cargo, undergone repairs and then reloaded. She sailed again for Malta and although she failed to arrive, she remained a symbol of the indomitable spirit of the Merchant Navy.

Chapter Seven

"By all us Big Steamers"

For the cause that lacks assistance,
For the wrong that needs resistance,
For the future in the distance,
And the good that I can do.
GEORGE LINNAEUS BANKS

THE LATE SUMMER OF 1942 AND THE FEW MONTHS FOLLOWING
marked what many regard as the fiercest phase of the U-boat
war. It is true that the development of long-range aircraft
was largely responsible for a new immunity enjoyed by Allied
shipping in the Western Approaches. But fresh submarines
were appearing in the "Wolf packs" and improvements in
the German supply system at sea enabled U-boats to operate
far away from their bases for longer periods.

News came of three more August sinkings, and in each case
the ship was far from land. The *Harmonides* went down in the
Indian Ocean when about 300 miles from Galle, the *Clan
Macnaughton* was sunk on the way to Trinidad and the *Clan
Macwhirter* met her end more than 200 miles from Madeira.
All these ships were torpedoed when proceeding alone,
clear evidence of the value of the convoy system at this
time.

Captain R. J. W. Bennet, of the *Macnaughton*, had expressed
surprise when his orders were changed for the second time and
he was told to sail for Trinidad, as it was known that a number

"Domestic news was exchanged by signals"

of ships were being sunk in that area. "I was informed that that was our route, so had no option but to comply with naval instructions," wrote the Master. He maintained a continuous zig-zag and had eight lookouts on duty, but neither submarine nor torpedo track was seen when his ship was hit. She sank in fifteen minutes with the loss of five lives.

The *Macwhirter* had the misfortune to be separated from her convoy by engine trouble and was torpedoed when doing her best to catch up. Captain R. S. Masters and nine of his men did not survive. After two shattering explosions, the Second Officer was heard shouting to the Master: "The ship has been torpedoed, sir." "I know that," was Captain Masters' cool answer as he made his way to the bridge and gave orders for the engines to be "rung off". As the *Macwhirter* went down by the stern he was seen walking from the starboard side of the lower bridge. Two boats were taken down with the ship and another capsized.

One Engineer Officer and twelve Indian sailors were lost in the *Harmonides*. The vessel was perpendicular in the water less than a quarter of an hour after being struck. In the few tense minutes during which it was possible to move about in the sinking ship, Captain H. Evans threw overboard the box containing confidential documents—a precaution faithfully taken by Masters almost without exception—gave orders to abandon ship, went to the wireless room with an additional distress message, walked along the deck to make sure that everybody had taken to the boats and took a last look at his ship from the bridge. The submarine that had made the attack did not surface.

The *Clan Macpherson*, which arrived in the Thames in September, 1942, brought accounts of enemy activity on the other side of the world. She had been in Sydney harbour at the time of the audacious attempt by the Japanese to penetrate the

defences with midget submarines. Captain Charles O'Byrne
reported that all the midget submarines were destroyed by the
harbour defence motor boats, using small depth charges.
Three of the under-water craft had not even managed to fire
their torpedoes, but one had torpedoed a ferry boat that was
being used as sleeping quarters for naval ratings, and had
caused loss of life. Captain O'Byrne also told of large Japanese
submarines shelling the Australian seaboard towns without
causing much damage. Four of the submarines had been
destroyed in about three weeks by aircraft operating off New
South Wales. The sea war was close enough to Australia to
cause all coastal shipping with speeds less than eleven knots to
be confined to convoy sailings.

The homeward run of the *Clan Macpherson* had been by way
of Panama and Halifax, with a variety of escorts. Two U.S.
destroyers and four armed motor patrol vessels, gave place to
two Canadian corvettes and two U.S. patrol vessels and these
were followed by two British trawlers and more Canadian Navy
escort ships. The U.S. Navy also provided strong air cover.
The Master of the *Macpherson* was pleasantly surprised to find
that the First Lieutenant of one of the British escort ships was
Lieut. Bedford, son of the then Managing Director of the Clan
Line. Domestic news was exchanged by signals which no
doubt mystified other ships in the convoy.

It was with clear satisfaction that Captain O'Byrne recorded
that with the convoy of sixty ships returning from Halifax
there sailed an auxiliary aircraft-carrier. "This vessel of about
10,000 tons," he wrote, "was a new, converted merchant ship.
She had on board six reconnaissance planes and about the same
number of fast fighter type aircraft. Only the former were
used. Soon after dawn each morning, about noon and again
towards sundown, a reconnaissance plane would leave the
carrier's deck and go away far ahead, to the sides and behind

the convoy on the look out for U-boats on the surface. On two occasions the convoy was turned as a result of this long-distance observation, I believe."

The *Clan Colquhoun* finished her twenty-first voyage when she sailed into Glasgow in mid-September, and provided yet another example of the great distances sailed and the remarkable carrying capacity of this type of merchant ship of about 8,000 tons gross. Her Master, Captain A. G. Storkey, gave this table of the mileage covered during a voyage which had lasted just over six months:

Liverpool to Cape Town .	7,594 miles
Cape Town to Durban . .	899 miles
Durban to Melbourne . .	5,554 miles
Melbourne to Sydney . .	642 miles
Sydney to Brisbane . .	639 miles
Brisbane to Gladstone . .	410 miles
Gladstone to Sydney . .	817 miles
Sydney to Lyttleton . .	1,493 miles
Lyttleton to Balboa . .	6,838 miles
Cristobel to Guantamano Bay .	763 miles
Guantamano to Key West .	734 miles
Key West to Newport . .	1,189 miles
Newport to Delaware . .	159 miles
Delaware to New York. .	151 miles
New York to Buzzard Bay .	168 miles
Buzzard Bay to Boston . .	71 miles
Boston to Halifax . .	382 miles
Halifax to the Clyde . .	2,500 miles

Figures, too, can speak for the carrying capacity of the *Clan Colquhoun*. Her homeward cargo was:

Loaded Brisbane:	40,080 boxes of butter
	2 cases of clothing
Loaded Gladstone:	23,980 boxes of butter
Loaded Sydney:	3 cases of naval stores
Loaded Lyttleton:	140,587 carcases of mutton
	10,824 packed goods
	1,187 sides of pork
	1,000 cases of preserved meat (not frozen)
Loaded Norfolk:	1,252 cases of frozen bacon
	2 cases of machinery
	240 pieces of oak plank
	166 bags of wood billets
	873 pieces of red oak (dunnage)
(on deck)	13 ambulances
(on deck)	18 cased trucks

From these figures one can at least get an idea of the immense value in goods alone when fifty or sixty ships steamed home in a single convoy. The mileage figures, coupled with the fact that the average speed of the *Clan Colquhoun* was around ten knots, give an impression of the watch-keeping strain imposed on Merchant Navy officers, particularly under war conditions.

Captain Storkey must be quoted on one other matter—the naval ratings and soldiers who found themselves turned into world voyagers in order that the guns of the merchant ships might have at least a nucleus of fully-trained men to man them. Of the *Colquhoun's* gunners Captain Storkey said: "These

The "Clan Lamont" in the Firth of Clyde.
1942.

men have been an example to the whole ship's company in their conduct, cleanliness and attention to duty. They practise every day with or without orders to do so."

Despite the enemy's big effort, the chances of getting through were still at least six to one, if the ships that were "in the news" in October, 1942, could be taken as a criterion. In that month, four Clan ships and the *Lanarkshire* arrived home, the *Clan Cameron* reported from her outward destination that she had missed being torpedoed by a few feet in an air attack and had fought off the plane when it came in for a second run, and the *Clan Mactavish* was torpedoed very shortly after picking up wounded survivors of another ship.

The *Lanarkshire* had taken out a full cargo of munitions, tanks, guns and aeroplanes to the Middle East, and had then made the long voyage to the River Plate. Two days, steaming from the Plate, there had been an encounter with a suspicious vessel whose funnel markings suggested that she belonged to a Swedish company. When first seen, the ship was on the port bow proceeding in the opposite direction. Carrying out instructions, Captain Matthews turned away and brought her astern. Instead of acting similarly, the other vessel turned off her course and followed the *Lanarkshire*. Maximum speed was ordered in the British ship, and then the stranger was lost in a rain squall.

Loaded to within two inches of her summer marks, the *Lanarkshire* only got out of the channel from Buenos Aires with difficulty. Two stranded vessels were passed, and later the Chief Engineer produced a bucket full of shells, stones and sea grass which had been taken from the condensers. Still, the *Lanarkshire* safely zig-zagged her way home on a course of over 7,200 miles laid down by the naval authorities.

First of the Clan ships to come in was the *Macdonald*, whose Master, Captain Parfitt, it will be remembered, had had to register a complaint about leaky phosgene gas bombs in his cargo at Karachi in June. Two cases of smallpox, which developed on the way to Australia, led to the Master and several of the crew being put into quarantine ashore for fourteen days. The ship, however, went on under the command of Chief Officer Woodall. Captain Parfitt was waiting to rejoin his ship when she arrived at Sydney. While there, the 6-inch gun, which had not been functioning properly, provided a further trial in the life of a peace-loving merchant Navy Master. With much forbearance, Captain Parfitt recorded that "a full naval gun's crew, under a gunnery Officer, was sent out to test the gun. The third shot fired nearly wrecked the gun . . ." (The dots are his.) The gun was landed, and later returned in good order.

The *Macbean*, *Macbrayne* and *Macarthur* arrived in United Kingdom ports within a few days of each other. The war had come closest to the *Macbean* on the outward passage to Cape Town. Picking up an S O S message from the S.S. *Cape Horn*, the *Macbean* altered course to go to her assistance. She found the *Cape Horn* burning fiercely, but the S.S. *Clifton Hall* was already on the scene and had taken off the crew. Told by signal that no further assistance was required, the *Macbean* altered course to get back on her ocean route. She had hardly done so when the *Cape Horn* blew up, the whole ship disappearing in a vast, heavy cloud of black smoke.

The *Macbrayne* went through "quite a lot of bombs" when steaming north after loading in the Royal Albert Dock, London, but subsequently had seven months of fairly uneventful sailing, if one disregards gales and monsoon weather and the normal difficulties of crowded ports in war-time.

As the Master, Captain J. McCrone, put it, "one thing after another," happened to the *Macarthur* as she sailed in convoy towards the Cape. First there was boiler trouble. Then the

Macarthur had to fall out of line for about an hour to investigate the reason for the starboard engine revolutions being much less than those of the port engine. Let Captain McCrone take up the story: "This stop seemed to worry the Senior Officer of the Escort in the cruiser *Mauritius*, who signalled me shortly afterwards to have a detailed signal sent to him as to the reason for our having to fall out. The locality, of course, was dangerous, to say the least of it. Up in position again, the steering gear jammed in the early hours of the morning. . . . However, I got the ship out of line again by means of the twin screws, and stopped until repairs had been effected, which did not take long. To me, this latter accident was the most unpleasant of all our worries up to that moment, especially as we were in convoy and steaming in somewhat tight formation. Lastly, gyro compass trouble developed. . . . For all of one night we had to steer by carrying an officer on the flying bridge, who steadied the ship on from time to time by the loom of the ship ahead of us."

Events at Durban, too, should be set down in Captain McCrone's forceful words. "On arrival at Durban (he wrote) it was decided by the Military on the one hand and the Ministry of War Transport on the other, that they wanted, perhaps, a dozen packages or so from us. To get these few items, they unlashed all our tanks in the 'tween decks, put them, and some 1,500 tons of other cargo, on shore, and then, of course, had to reload the same amount, making a total of cargo handled of some 3,000 tons deadweight. Expense does not seem to enter into anyone's calculations when a ship is on charter to the Government, although what was of more interest to me at the time was that all our tanks, which had been beautifully secured at home, were all unlashed, and we had a passage facing us around Socotra in the height of the monsoon. However, although the usual frantic rush developed at the last moment to get us away, everything was put back approximately as it was in the first place. The monsoon was very heavy, but nothing moved in the holds."

The eventful nature of the *Macarthur's* voyage continued in evidence after her arrival at Suez. There was an explosion in No. 2 hold while ammunition was being discharged. Again the common-sense view of a typical British Merchant Navy Master should be quoted. "The 25-pounder shells which exploded in No. 2 hold were stowed on their own," Captain McCrone stated, "but the same type of ammunition was stowed in No. 4 lower hold up against a number of 4,000 lb. bombs. While I realise the impossibility of making things one hundred per cent safe with this type of cargo, I do think that it is hardly the thing to put relatively small calibre ammunition, which is apt to be treated with some degree of 'familiarity' but which, in view of our own experience, can explode and do damage in spite of an alleged triple safety device, in close proximity to 4,000 lb. bombs, which have to be dealt with with the greatest care and do not permit of any degree of carelessness in their handling."

The *Macarthur* steamed on to the River Plate, but apart from some bouts of boiler tube trouble, her progress was not marked by any untoward event.

The circumstances of the sinking of the *Clan Mactavish*, the ship that did *not* get home in October, 1942, present in full the barbarous nature of the unrestricted sea warfare as waged by the Germans. The *Mactavish* (her proud record included a successful fight with an enemy surface raider in the 1914–18 War) had been away nearly twelve months on very useful service in the Middle East and the Indian Ocean. To a cargo of 4,600 tons of copper she had added a thousand tons of general cargo at Durban. She was to make her way home via New York.

The *Mactavish* had headed into the South Atlantic (her approximate position was 35.20 S.; 16.30 E.) when, at 4 a.m. on October 8, the Chief Officer sighted a light ahead. Eyes strained into the darkness and presently the light, which was taken to be that of a torch, flickered on and off to make the letters "S O S". The *Mactavish* was sailing alone in an area which was generally considered safe. Routeing instructions were that dimmed navigation lights should be used to ten degrees east. But the Germans had been known to take advantage even of the universally accepted "Save Our Souls" appeal, and the Master of the *Mactavish*, Captain E. E. Arthur, decided that he must stand off for the short time that remained before dawn. In about an hour it was light enough for those looking out anxiously from the Clan ship to see a lifeboat under sail. Steps were at once taken to get those in it on board. Then a second boat was seen, and by 7.30 a.m. the *Mactavish* had picked up thirty-five survivors of the ex-Danish vessel *Boringia*, which had been torpedoed just after midnight. It was indeed a mercy rescue because a number of the survivors were injured, including a stewardess.

One is forced to the conclusion that the efforts of the British crew were watched through a periscope because the weather was fine and clear and the *Mactavish*, whose maximum speed at the time was under ten knots, was herself torpedoed well within the hour, when she had turned in her tracks and was doing her best to get the injured survivors to Cape Town. The casualties from the previous torpedoing were being attended to in the saloon of the *Mactavish* at the very moment the torpedo struck. Water was bubbling out of the deep tank ventilators within a few minutes and the ship quickly reared up to make her final head-first plunge. Boats were cut away, but as men jumped overboard the inrushing waters flung them back amidships. Many of them were dragged deep down by the suction of the sinking ship, and when the turmoil subsided the half-drowned survivors of two ships were left clinging to odd bits of wreckage in sight of two up-turned and damaged life-boats.

They were found sometime later by an aircraft which, after a lapse of hours, led a rescue ship to them. Of the crew of ninety-one of the *Clan Mactavish*, only thirty-seven survived, and Captain Arthur was not among them. Seven of the thirty-five souls they had tried to save were also lost.

The *Clan Macinnes*—the ship that had had the strange encounter with a dhow and submarine seven months earlier—arrived in the Clyde at the beginning of November, 1942. She had been through a heavy Japanese air raid on Trincomalee, during which one enemy plane dived into an oil tank and started a conflagration which lasted for two days. In August she had kept close company with a U-boat for a very short time. The *Macinnes* was then on the way to Port of Spain. The U-boat surfaced in the early evening, only about 500 yards from the British merchantman. Apparently the submarine was as surprised as the British ship, because she immediately submerged again. Very heavy rain and nightfall enabled the *Macinnes* to escape. "I kept the *Macinnes* in the blackest patches, and proceeded at utmost speed," Captain Lynch stated.

He was prepared to admit that when, two days later, after passing through wreckage and oil, he saw two small objects low in the water he thought "the hour had come". The gunners of the *Macinnes* closed up for action as the objects were put astern. "The order had almost been given to fire," and then the dots on the water four or five miles away from the *Macinnes* were identified as lifeboats. Thirty-five men, several of them badly burned, from an American ship which had been torpedoed two nights previously, were rescued.

No doubt the British Master was shaken by the thought that

he might unwittingly have opened fire on these poor men, because he wrote later: "The experience firmly convinces me that, at a distance, and with certain atmospheric conditions prevailing, a lifeboat, with a lug sail set, looks suspiciously like a U-boat with conning tower above water." Yet what Master could afford to wait to confirm or disprove a doubt, when his adversary was seldom even a speck on the ocean?

In the middle of November, the *Clan Mactaggart*, which had played a particularly useful part in conveying troops, stores and ammunition for the North Africa landings, was sunk owing to a sequence of unfortunate circumstances. Going into Gibraltar, some necessary engine repairs were started, and then orders were suddenly given to Captain J. H. Crellin to take the *Mactaggart* out with a convoy that was just sailing. The ship was got under way as soon as possible, a signal having been made to the naval authorities ashore. On a clear moonlight night, the *Mactaggart* proceeded at thirteen knots in an attempt to overtake the convoy. Captain Crellin expected to sight it before midnight, but a radio message had altered the course of the convoy. As a result, the *Mactaggart* passed it to the southward in the darkness. Meanwhile, a corvette, which was to have escorted the *Mactaggart*, although Captain Crellin had not been informed of the arrangement, was held up temporarily at the boom.

Just before dawn, when the unescorted merchantman was sixteen miles from the main convoy and about ninety-two miles from the Cape Tarifa Light, she was torpedoed. Of 178 persons in the *Mactaggart* at the time, 175 survived and were picked up by the corvette that should have been their escort. Captain Crellin himself was knocked over the ship's side while helping to release a lifeboat, and noted later, with some bitterness, that he lost £100 from the Canteen Fund as a consequence.

Two pertinent points were raised following the loss of the *Mactaggart*:

1. Should the merchantman have been allowed to sail without the corvette escort?
2. Was it advisable to order the *Mactaggart* to attempt to catch up with the convoy when it was obvious that there would be submarines in the vicinity, and when it was reasonable to suppose that there would be other convoys returning from the expedition in the near future?

What official answers, if any, were given to these questions, I cannot say. It was Oscar Wilde who declared that: "Experience is the name everyone gives to his mistakes," and there is no doubt that much bitter experience was needed before we won a great war.

A remarkable rescue record was established by the *Clan Alpine* (Captain C. W. Banbury) during November. It was the *Alpine*, it will be recalled, that carried 1,000 men, women and children to safety from Batavia (Chapter Six). At the beginning of November, when on passage from Lourenço Marques to Port Elizabeth, she was guided by an aircraft to the rescue of fifty-six survivors of a British ship who had been in their boats for a little over a day. Less than three weeks later, when far out in the South Atlantic, the *Alpine* picked up three boat-loads of exhausted survivors from the liner *City of Cairo*. There were eleven children, the youngest only thirteen months old, among the 150 souls in these boats. They had been adrift for nearly a fortnight and were suffering from thirst, hunger and bad sunburn. They were so weak that it was only with the utmost difficulty that they could be got on board the *Alpine*. Every man in the Clan ship not on watch or required for some other duty, joined the Chief Steward's first aid parties, but two In-

dians died before St. Helena was reached. Captain Banbury
paid tribute to the fine navigation of Captain Rogerson and
the officers of the *City of Cairo*, in bringing the boats to within
sixty miles of St. Helena, but was stating no more than the cold
truth when he said: "Many of the survivors had reached the
end of their endurance and would not have lived another
twenty-four hours. Two more died in hospital before we left
port."

Survivors from a Brazilian steamer were picked up by the
Clan Macgillivray on her way to Trinidad only a few days later.
The *Macgillivray*, 6,464 tons gross, only stopped twenty
minutes to take on board twenty-seven men. They were landed
next day at Port of Spain.

On Christmas Day, 1942, the *Clan Macneil* made fast in the
Royal Albert Dock, London, ready for discharge. It was just
one more home-coming after a long and uneventful voyage.
She had been to the Middle East, had experienced monsoon
weather and Atlantic gales and had more than once been
Commodore's ship. But Captain A. Macniven had little to
report beyond his fuel consumption and the distances sailed
between ports of call. He did mention that in rough weather
on the way to Colombo, the deck head of the deep tank burst,
but was only concerned to underline the fact that "no cargo
was damaged".

Last of the Clan ships to come home in 1942 were the *Murdoch* and the *Macnair*. Both had suffered damage in heavy
Atlantic weather, and lifeboats had been smashed or washed
away. "The weather reached its climax on the night of the
20th December," Captain McPherson, of the *Macnair* said,
"when we were steaming beam on to a full north-westerly
gale, and with a tremendous beam sea. In freezing conditions,
the ship rolled very heavily through an arc of seventy degrees.
All saloon and midship accommodation was flooded, pantry

and office doors were stove in and the port ladder from the lower bridge was carried away. . . ."

With both admiration and gratitude, he added that one of the small ships of the Navy's escort rammed a U-boat, despite the weather, on Boxing Day.

Arriving in the Clyde on the morning of New Year's Day, 1943, was the Clan operated S.S. *Lieut. St. Loubert Bie* (Captain Pengelly). Moving up from the sunny South, she too, had experienced atrocious weather on the last lap of her voyage across the Atlantic. With the temperature twelve or more degrees below freezing, everything was covered with icicles. For eleven consecutive days, including Christmas, the wind blew at gale force, blinding snow accompanying the squalls. One of the able seamen died and was buried at sea in a raging blizzard. On Christmas Eve, when about 300 miles off Cape Farewell, Greenland, two cracks appeared in the upper deck plating to add to Captain Pengelly's troubles. But the ship came in safely after more than eight months of voyaging, and it is hardly surprising—for there had been many worries before the Atlantic was crossed—that the Master should conclude his long report: "I shall be very grateful for a rest and a change, if at all convenient."

The *Clan Macbrayne*, outward bound, had two very narrow escapes early in January when attacked by torpedo-carrying aircraft. A torpedo was fired at the stern of the *Macbrayne*, but Captain Paull quickly marked its track. By putting his helm hard-a-port, he was able to get clear by ten feet. Almost before anyone on board could get his breath back, a second torpedo was spotted, this time heading for the bows of the vessel. Again Captain Paull went hard-a-port but, in his own words: "this time I was not sure whether or not it would hit the vessel until it had actually slipped by."

Unhappily, the torpedo that was aimed at the *Clan Mac-*

fadyen gave her no chance of escape. Struck amidships, she broke her back and sank in ninety seconds with the loss of seventy-nine lives. It was in the New Year that statements from the very few survivors were obtained, although the *Macfadyen* had gone to her doom on November 26, when about 100 miles from Port of Spain.

The Master, Captain P. Williams, and most of the officers were lost, but Mr. J. Dick, Fifth Engineer, was able to tell how the ship sank before any of the boats could be got away. He himself had climbed on to a raft as it was floating away from the top of No. 4 Hatch. One other raft floated clear. On these rafts, the Third Engineer, the Fifth Engineer, Seaman-Gunner John Beattie, Apprentice Paul Stevens, an Army gunner and a handful of the Indian crew, clung to life for six days. Then they were seen by an aircraft, and a rescue vessel was sent to pick them up. To close this tragic episode, the survivors told how the U-boat surfaced after the *Macfadyen* had disappeared and passed very close to them *but took no notice.* . . .

> "To count the life of battle good
>   And dear the land that gave you birth,
>   And dearer yet the brotherhood
>   That binds the brave of all the earth". . .

Such callousness puts men outside the brotherhood envisaged by Newbolt.

During the first few weeks of 1943, ships came in from various parts of the world. The *Clan Macinnes* had had a fairly exciting trip to Algeria, and the *Macgillivray* more than a taste of bombing in Colombo and bad weather in many widely separated sea areas. The *Macbean*, too, had been to Algeria, where she passed unharmed through a bombing that went on spasmodically for all of an otherwise pleasant moonlight night.

The *Macaulay*, sailing alone, had successfully evaded a U-boat that surfaced only six miles away from her, and the *Banffshire*, in convoy, was just as lucky during three night attacks by U-boats.

One more fine modern cargo liner was lost—the *Clan Chattan*. Set on fire by bombing while attempting to get supplies through to Malta from the eastern end of the Mediterranean, she had to be abandoned. Her Master, Captain M. H. Jones, practically all her crew and more than 200 troops and naval ratings who had been taking passage in her, were rescued by naval vessels.

When the *Perthshire* appeared in the Clyde in mid-February, she had completed a voyage of 32,100 miles in 295 days, 13 hours and 42 minutes. She had called at more ports than can be mentioned on her way across the world and back. Her experiences included a collision in Australian waters, which, happily, did not result in injury or loss of life, and a night encounter with a U-boat which surfaced so close to the *Perthshire* that it was impossible for the enemy to fire a torpedo without blowing himself out of the water!

*"We were steaming beam on
to a full north west gale"*

Chapter Eight

Menace in the Skies

There is no danger seamen have not run!
Tempests have drowned them since the world began.
They have dared shipwreck, frost-bite and the sun,
But they have dared a greater danger, Man.

JOHN MASEFIELD

AMONG THE MANY SHIPS OF THE CLAN FLEET TO COMPLETE
voyages in the latter half of the fourth year of war was the *Clan
Forbes*. She had been away since June, 1941, and her special
service at Addu Atoll and elsewhere has already been described.
This had continued until the beginning of 1943; and even after
the ship had been in drydock at Bombay for a quick overhaul,
there were indications that the authorities were loath to part
with such an efficient and useful unit as the *Clan Forbes*. She
was suddenly requisitioned again to carry 2,000 tons of Government stores urgently needed in Mombasa. These were discharged early in February and the *Clan Forbes* was at last free
to load a normal cargo and head for home. She coaled and
stored at Cape Town on March 7, received orders at sea to join
a fast convoy at Gibraltar and was in the Mersey on April 5.

.   .   .   .   .   .

March to September, 1943, represented one of the strangest
periods in the whole war-long battle at sea. It opened on a note
of crisis, with more than a hundred U-boats known to be at
sea. They were operating from the Arctic to the wide expanses

of the Indian Ocean. In March alone we lost 108 ships with a total of more than 600,000 tons. In April, the figures had dropped to fifty-six ships and 320,000 tons, and in May, to fifty ships and 265,000 tons. More U-boat "kills" were taking place, and there were indications of two very important trends:

1. That the offensive was no longer with the enemy, and,
2. That the general standard of U-boat Commanders and crews was deteriorating.

In June and July, the famous submarine hunter, Captain F. J. Walker, D.S.O., R.N., in command of the Second Escort Group, introduced new methods of attack, and the enemy suffered heavily in the Bay of Biscay. Our aircraft, particularly those of Coastal Command, operated with even more deadly effect—in six weeks they sank twenty-one U-boats—but the Germans, too, were making full use of long-range aircraft against our shipping.

Much could be written of the immensely valuable services rendered by the host of Clan ships that safely came and went during this period of improvement. But that, like so much more that the Merchant Navy did during the war, must be taken for granted—and not ungratefully so—while we tell the stories of four ships that did not get through. In one case air attack was directly responsible for the loss, in another it was an important contributory cause, and in a third, the lack of air cover was questioned.

Captain Crellin, who had been torpedoed in the *Clan Mac-taggart* less than four months earlier, took the *Clan Alpine* to sea on March 6, 1943. On the sixth day out, an enemy aircraft passed over the convoy and dropped a few bombs without doing any damage. But the scent had been picked up and, no doubt, passed to the U-boat pack. Before dawn next day, four ships in the convoy had been torpedoed, including the *Clan Alpine*. The explosion aft had the unfortunate effect of causing the poop deck to collapse into the crew's quarters. The 4-inch gun was also brought down and jammed several doors. Two gunners who were stationed on the gun platform were blown off but in some amazing manner escaped serious injury. Trapped in their quarters, twenty-six Indian ratings were not so lucky; they were either killed outright or drowned before they could get clear.

Four boats got away from the *Alpine* with sixty-eight survivors, including Captain Crellin. Their position was about 190 miles west of Cape Finisterre. When daylight came two hours later, the survivors were picked up by the naval sloop *Scarborough*, and it was seen that the *Alpine* was still afloat although down by the stern. Captain Crellin at once asked the Commander of the Navy ship to put him back on board his own vessel so that a final search could be made for survivors. With a Sub-Lieutenant and three naval ratings, the Master climbed on board his stricken ship, but after fifteen minutes he was satisfied that nobody remained alive in her.

While the party made their grim search, an enemy aircraft appeared on the scene but was driven off by gunfire from H.M.S. *Scarborough*. But once again, what otherwise would have remained hidden, had been revealed by air reconnaisance, and the party was recalled to the sloop. There continued the question of what to do with the big merchantman, still afloat but with her after deck under water.

It was more than probable that German submarines were still in the vicinity and, in any case, enemy bases were not far away. The convoy, too, had been left with only five escort ships, a corvette having been detached at the same time as the *Scarborough*. It was not a pleasant decision to have to make in the presence of the Master of a proud ship, but the naval Commander had his duty to do and, rather than risk the *Clan Alpine* falling into the hands of the enemy, two depth charges were fired against the side of the vessel abreast of the engine-room. In four minutes she sank, taking with her the brave men from far-off India who had already given their lives in a great cause.

Six weeks elapsed before the *Clan Macpherson* was sunk in the Gulf of Guinea in rather disquieting circumstances. On her way home from India, her cargo included 2,750 tons of pig iron, 3,120 tons of ground nuts and hundreds of tons of linseed, jute and tea. Built in 1929, she had a winter deadweight capacity of more than 10,000 tons. Her voyage had been like so many others—an early winter battering in the Atlantic, moderate north-east Trade winds on the way to the Cape, a call at Colombo and then on to Madras and Calcutta. Returning, she had left Cape Town as "Commodore ship" of a lightly-protected convoy and had been diverted to Takoradi in mid-April.

The *Macpherson* was still "Commodore vessel" when the convoy, which had swollen to nineteen ships, sailed from Takoradi on the morning of April 26, with an escort of one corvette and three trawlers. With foreboding, her Master, Captain E. Gough, noted that there was no air cover. Three days out, Captain Gough received a message from the Senior Officer of the Escort that the convoy was being shadowed by submarines, and during the night three evasive courses were ordered. On the next day, April 30, one aeroplane was seen at 9.30 a.m. and another at 4 p.m. An Asdic "contact" had been reported by the escort shortly before midday and an emergency turn was carried out by the convoy.

A truly catastrophic night followed. The weather, according to Captain Gough's report, was "fine, clear and overcast" when the first ship of the convoy was torpedoed at 8.55 p.m.

Within five minutes, three more had been hit. Course was altered twice in the next four hours and then, at 3.40 a.m., the U-pack launched another onslaught and three more ships were torpedoed in five minutes, the *Clan Macpherson* being the last of them. With his ship settling down by the head, Captain Gough gave orders to abandon ship and stand by until daylight. The Master highly praised his officers and men for their excellent conduct while getting the boats away, and Apprentice Wehner was singled out for special mention.

After pulling away from the *Macpherson*, the Fourth Officer's boat was hailed by the S.S. *Silver Ash* and those in the boat were taken on board. The other five boats of the *Macpherson* kept in touch by flashlight during the hours of darkness. At about 6 a.m., the escort trawler *Arran* came up and asked if Captain Gough and his men wished to be taken on board. The first light, however, had shown that the *Macpherson* was still afloat and Captain Gough therefore declined the offer but asked the naval vessel to stand by as he proposed to re-board his ship.

An hour later, the Master was back on board the *Macpherson* with the 130 officers and men who had spent half the night in five lifeboats. A survey was made and it was found that No. 2 hold was full of water up to the shelter deck, and Nos. 1 and 3 holds were dry. This information was passed by signal to the escort and Captain Gough intimated that he would try to get his ship into port under her own steam. All the engineers went below and commenced to raise steam, while the Deck Officers saw that boats were hove into place, coiled falls and also took sights to verify the ship's position. The *Clan Macpherson* became a living thing again.

It was realised that when the vessel began to make headway, the water in No. 2 hold would surge over the shade deck coamings and would run forward along the shelter deck to

No. 1 hold. Arrangements were made to put the pumps on to No. 1 hold as soon as the ship was under way. The fire salvage pumps were rigged as an additional safeguard. At 9.20 a.m., the engines were put "Ahead" to twenty revolutions and the ship was turned on to a course for Freetown, sixty-seven miles away. Continuous soundings were taken of No. 1 hold and it was found that the water had risen quickly to a depth of six feet. In twenty-five minutes it became necessary to stop the engines and fill No. 4 tank to correct a list to starboard.

Captain Gough then signalled to the escort vessel to pick up his tow-wire, with the intention of having the *Macpherson* towed stern first. At about 10 a.m., the ship was listing to starboard, with a freeboard of roughly three feet abreast of No. 1 hold, where the water was still rising. The engine-room telegraph was put to "Finish with engines" and the engineers below were told to be in readiness for the towing operation.

For the events of the next quarter of an hour, which were to have tragic results, I will turn to the Report subsequently made to the owners by Captain Gough. "At 10.10 a.m.," he stated, "the vessel took a further list to starboard, causing the sea to lap over on to the fore deck, No. 1 bulkhead apparently having carried away. I immediately gave the order to abandon ship, and at the same moment I myself telephoned to the engine-room giving the order to abandon ship. All four boats were in the water and pulling away from the vessel at 10.13 a.m. The *Clan Macpherson* sank at 10.15 a.m."

And the tragic outcome of the courageous attempt to save the merchantman and her cargo was contained in the next paragraph of the Master's statement: "It is now with very great regret that I report the loss of Chief Engineer Robertson, Second Engineer Marshall, Fourth Engineer MacMurtrie and Fifth Engineer Cunningham, who went down with their vessel. After the vessel disappeared at 10.15, the area was carefully searched for possible survivors, both by my own motor launch and also by the boats of H.M.S. *Arran*. All survivors were taken on board H.M.S. *Arran*, and we left the scene of the disaster at 12.15 p.m., setting course for Freetown."

Eight hours later, the survivors arrived in Freetown harbour, and there was nothing about their reception calculated to lift the shadow cast by the loss of the gallant Engineer Officers. Captain Gough and his men were not put ashore until an hour before midnight. They were then given two sandwiches and a glass of cold cordial each and went to sleep without the opportunity of a wash. On the following day, Captain Gough lodged a complaint with the Senior Naval Officer on behalf of all the Masters in the convoy, on the inadequate escort and lack of air protection afforded to the convoy.

These, and other points, were taken up subsequently by the Chamber of Shipping of the United Kingdom and the owners. Commander N. D. Holbrook, V.C., R.N., Casualty Section (Trade Division), the Admiralty, asked for further particulars of the sinking of the *Macpherson*, and Captain Gough provided details which must have won the admiration of a holder of the highest award for gallantry. The Master revealed that the Chief Engineer and his staff went down to the engine-room although the extent of the damage below deck could not be ascertained. Bags of ground nuts were spread over No. 1 shelter deck. The Chief, Second and Third Officers, Apprentice Wehner and several Indian members of the crew, volunteered to build the bags into a temporary bulkhead. "They worked in water up to their knees, regardless of danger, their only thought being to save their ship and her valuable cargo," Captain Gough wrote. Commander Holbrook no doubt agreed when the Master added: "No praise is too high for the courageous spirit and dauntless devotion to duty which was shown by my officers, engineers and volunteer crew in their magnificent attempt to save their ship."

Complaints regarding the strength and speed of the escort— it was alleged by Captain Gough that the trawlers could do little more than eight knots—were conveyed to the Director of Trade Division, the Admiralty, by Mr. F. Bedford, on behalf of the owners. In his letter he said: "The reason I am writing you is that a very strong feeling exists that many of these vessels [in the convoy], if not all, have been needlessly sacrificed." He mentioned the lack of air cover and raised these questions:

1. Whether, knowing there were submarines on the track of this convoy, it was not possible for destroyers to be sent out from Freetown to give the necessary protection, and,

2. Whether the courses which the convoy was instructed to take were, in the circumstances, proper ones.

Replying, the Director wrote: "I fully appreciate your distress at the loss of such a fine ship, which I can assure you is shared by all of us at the Admiralty. We are, as you can understand, bound to consider the U-boat war as a whole and view each incident in its right perspective. The U-boat threat, for instance, off the West African coast is but a fraction of that in the North Atlantic and we obviously must allocate our limited resources in escort vessels accordingly. Were it possible, there is nothing we would like better than to give every convoy a really strong escort."

The letter further stated that if there had been any additional escort vessels available for the convoy, they would have been sent. Trawlers, similar to those in the escort, were employed as anti-submarine escorts in many parts of the world and, whilst not as good as destroyers or corvettes, had done useful work.

The course of the convoy was in every way a proper one and, with regard to aircraft, visibility at the time was very poor.

"It is our opinion, confirmed by experience," the Director concluded, "that a convoy with even only a weak surface escort, affords better protection to merchant ships than if they are sailed singly unescorted. Our views are supported by the fact that during the last twelve months, 650 ships have sailed in these convoys between Freetown and Takoradi with a loss of only eleven, i.e., 1.7 per cent. Whilst I have no wish to minimise the seriousness of the losses sustained on this occasion, war invariably leads to blows and counter-blows, and it would be illogical not to expect the enemy occasionally to get in a nasty punch. I can only assure you that we are fully alive to all the risks which have to be run and we are deploying our forces to the best of our ability to bring about the ultimate defeat of the U-boat."

The matter was not allowed to rest there. A further report was called for from Captain Gough and the loss of the *Clan Macpherson* became a subject on the agenda of the Shipping Defence Advisory Committee of the Admiralty. Acknowledging the letter of the Director, Trade Division, Mr. Bedford said: "The views of the Masters of the vessels lost are more bitter than I have known to exist on any previous occasion."

Complaints regarding the treatment of the *Clan Macpherson* survivors in Freetown elicited the following from the Ministry of War Transport: "It has to be admitted that the arrangements in Freetown were not good in that, in spite of all the efforts which had been made, they were unable to cope with the big rush of personnel landed in that area all about the same time. . . . Very active steps are being taken."

The after events of the sinking of the *Clan Macpherson* have been described at some length as an example of the vast amount of careful, thoughtful work that had to go on behind the scenes in order that ships could do their vital war-time duties speedily and efficiently. Every Master and every man would have supported Mr. Bedford in writing to the Admiralty: "I know full well that what has happened cannot be undone, but I would like to feel that the lessons of this unhappy episode are not being lost, and to have assurance that proper steps are being taken to obviate such an occurrence in the future, so far as is possible."

We now come to an amazing feature of the four sinkings that took place in the fleets of the Clan and associate Lines during the six months to September, 1943. First of the vessels, as has been so recently described, was the *Clan Alpine*, which Captain Crellin took to sea after he had been torpedoed in another ship only four months earlier. In mid-July, four months again from the time of the loss of the *Alpine*, he sailed from Glasgow in command of the S.S. *Halizones* of the Houston Line, bound for Montevideo and Buenos Aires. And ten days later, before his ship was clear of the outward convoy, he was for the third time in less than a year compelled to give the grim order: "Abandon Ship."

Aerial bombing accounted for the *Halizones*, and this is the story of her end, more or less in Captain Crellin's own words. She left the Clyde in Convoy O.S. 52, her convoy number being 115. There were sixty-seven ships in the convoy and the escort consisted of six or seven corvettes and sloops and one frigate. The weather was fine and clear with light to moderate variable winds. There was no attack on the convoy until July 26, when four Focke-Wulf Condors came over at 9,000 to 10,000 feet in the early evening. They dropped sticks of bombs, and after being "near missed" No. 121, a motor vessel, was hit by three bombs and sank in thirteen minutes. Five minutes later No. 14 was "near missed" and, with her engine-room flooded, was taken in tow by a tug which headed for Lisbon. There was no more enemy action that day.

The alarm for further air attacks was given at 7.20 next morning, and very shortly afterwards the first Focke-Wulf was seen flying in from astern of the convoy. As this plane gained height, four more were detected at varying altitudes. At 10,000 feet there was thin, patchy cloud and the five aircraft circled the convoy for a time. They made their first attack at about 8 a.m., dropping three sticks of bombs, all of which went close to No. 103 without doing serious damage to the vessel. Emergency turns had been ordered by flag signals but, twenty minutes later, bombs dropped close to the ship next astern of the *Halizones*.

Then, after another thirty-five minutes of anxious watching, it was the turn of the *Halizones* herself. The ship was coming round to port and steadying on a new course when an enemy plane came in on the starboard side. Flying at about 10,000 feet, the aircraft was at first in cloud. When it could be properly seen, the *Halizones* went into action with guns and rockets, but although the shooting was accurate, it was very short.

Captain Crellin and Second Officer F. C. Chisholm then saw four bombs coming towards the *Halizones*. It seemed certain that they must hit but, growing larger as they screamed through the air, they appeared to spread out. Two fell close by the starboard side of the bridge and two on the port side by the engine-room. How miraculous was the escape of the *Halizones* from a direct hit may be judged from the fact that one of the bombs cut the stern off No. 4 lifeboat as it grazed past the ship into the sea. But although she had missed a direct hit, it was at once obvious that the ship had suffered grave injury from the explosions. For a time she was hidden in a great cloud of smoke, dust and water. Plastic armour and cement blocks around the bridge were torn down, both compasses were smashed and more damage was done as the vessel tossed violently in the aftermath of the explosions. In the engine-room, the main injection was fractured completely, causing a strong flow of water which it was impossible to stop. The ballast pump and other important units, were put out of action. The only pump in order was the main engine circulating pump. The dynamo was still running but all lights had gone out. The wireless room was wrecked.

When it was possible to see anything in or on the ship again, Captain Crellin stopped the engines and made a hasty examination. Nos. 2 and 3 holds had commenced to make water. He gave the order to abandon ship but quickly countermanded it. The Second Officer returned to the bridge with the news that there was no hope of going full speed ahead to rejoin the convoy as the engines could not be re-started. The situation of the *Halizones* was desperate indeed because two enemy aircraft still hovered over her in her crippled state. A frigate of the escort closed with her and opened fire on them.

At 9.10 a.m. Captain Crellin, for the second time, gave the order to abandon. Whatever he may have thought of his own luck, his crew had been lucky and not one man had suffered injury. By 9.20 they were clear of the ship, which had a marked list to starboard, and the boats were ordered to keep well away in case further bombs came down. The Master then went all over the ship. In the engine-room, he found the water above the starboard side of the starting platform. At 9.40 he re-appeared on deck and waved the Second Officer alongside to take him off in the motor boat. On board the frigate, he explained the situation to the naval Commander, but when it was suggested that the *Halizones* might be towed, Captain Crellin at once led a party of officers, engineers and "Dems" gunners back to the ship. While the D.E.M.S. ratings manned the guns and the Chief Officer, on the forecastle, prepared to take the tow, the Master and Chief Engineer surveyed the chaos in the engine-room. The water was still creeping up and as it was impossible to start the engines there was no way of keeping it down or pumping it out. The carpenter, who had been sounding the holds, reported seventeen inches of water in No. 1, four feet six inches in No. 2 and five feet in No. 3.

Efforts were still being made to get the towing wire on board the *Halizones* when the Captain of the frigate ordered Captain Crellin and his men to abandon their ship for the second time. The order had been passed to the frigate by signal from the Senior Officer of the Escort, who required the waiting warship to help guard the onward-steaming convoy. Once again it was the end, but Captain Crellin made no mention of his own incredibly bitter experiences in his subsequent report. Instead, he commended the cool efficiency of Second Officer Chisholm as gunnery director, and mentioned that, in the two attacks, sixteen pans of oerlikon ammunition and fifty 2-inch rockets were fired.

The *Clan Macarthur*, one of the largest ships of the Clan fleet, was sunk in the Indian Ocean in August after a particularly cold-blooded night attack by a submarine. The first torpedo struck without warning, and as the crew prepared to get away in the boats, two more torpedoes were fired into the merchantman, causing considerable loss of life.

The *Macarthur* was alone, the convoy out of Durban having dispersed three days earlier. Captain J. D. Matthews was maintaining a continual zig-zag and the ship was just beginning to turn to starboard when, twenty-five minutes after moonset, the first big explosion came. Before the second torpedo hit the ship, he was able to visit the wireless room, where Senior Operator R. G. Cole was sending out an S O S, and order all secret codes and papers to be collected and placed in the large weighted box, ready for dumping over the side. The first torpedo had struck well aft and a number of Indian members of the crew were killed or injured while others were trapped. Chief Engineer Currie, Mr. Ruthven, Chief Steward Taylor and Surgeon Ungr went to the aid of these men. Three of them were not among the survivors. "From accounts given to me," Captain Matthews wrote later, "it would appear that Currie, Taylor and Ungr could have saved themselves but very gallantly chose to help others, and in so doing lost their lives."

When the second torpedo struck amidships, it demolished all three port lifeboats and the motor boat. Some men had already climbed into the boats. The Master sent Apprentice Lindsay down to release the safety pins on all rafts, and then paid a second visit to the wireless room. He found it completely wrecked but Senior Operator Cole, although hurt and dazed, was still struggling to get another S O S away on the emergency set.

"He assured me that he had got the message away and had had an acknowledgment from Lourenço Marques, which was a great relief to me," Captain Matthews recorded. "After commending him, I sent him to his boat, and had no sooner done so than the third torpedo struck. This was quickly followed by a terrific downfall of hatches and heavy debris. I decided: 'It's time for us to leave her' and told the Second Officer to get into the boat and hang on a bit for me."

With the ship on fire and sinking by the stern, the Master went to his room, "or, rather the entrance", and picked up his ditty bag and lifebelt. He then shouted in the darkness for any member of his crew that might still be capable of getting away from the ship but received no answer. He went down a life-line into the only boat alongside. Almost at once, the *Clan Macarthur* took her final plunge, and in the midst of that holocaust, the Master did not fail to note with surprise that the ship went head-first under the waters.

The boat in which Captain Matthews found himself was crowded much beyond capacity, and water was steadily rising in it. He feared that the bottom had been stove-in by an underwater explosion which had taken place as the *Macarthur* sank. Men scrambled in the water to find the leaks, and to the great relief of all it was discovered that only the plug in the bottom of the boat had been blown out. A fresh one was inserted and efforts were being made to bale the water out of the boat when there came the most fantastic experience of the whole of that terrible night.

The Second Officer, who was looking out ahead of the boat, suddenly shouted: "Submarine emerging right in our track," and the next minute the crowded boat was bumping along the bulges of the U-boat. Three oars were broken in a desperate attempt to keep away from the submarine which threatened to capsize the boat. Men appeared on the forward part of the U-boat (Apprentice Lindsay declared that he saw a "U" on the conning tower, although it was too dark to see any number) and there was a rapid fire of questions. They were not answered by Captain Matthews because he, with no desire to be made prisoner, had ducked under the thwarts and lay in the water at the bottom of the boat. During the questioning, which was mainly concerned with the name of the ship and where she had come from and where she was going, one of the survivors flashed a torch. From the conning tower there came the peremptory order: "Light out, quick." This was followed by: "Look out for propellers—I go," and the U-boat slid away as suddenly as she had appeared.

Captain Matthews estimated that the U-boat was more than 200 feet along. She had a fairly heavy gun ahead of the conning tower and powerful anti-aircraft armament.

When daylight came, the men packed in Captain Matthews' boat were cheered by the sight of two other lifeboats, more or less full, and several rafts. Contact was made and, following a roll call, it was found that seven Europeans and forty-five Indians were missing. It was decided to remain in the vicinity as help might be expected to follow on the reception of the S O S sent out before the *Macarthur* sank. The survivors were distributed more evenly among the boats, and water and provisions from five rafts were shared. Then the rafts were cast adrift as they were inclined to bump and damage the boats. "With the extra water tanks and provisions we were ready for the long sail to Madagascar if it became necessary," the Master stout-heartedly declared. Happily it was not necessary, although the survivors were compelled to spend one more cold and cramped night in the boats.

Fairly early on the morning following the sinking, they were sighted by a Catalina flying-boat which flew round and made the signal: "Cheer up, help is coming," but did not say when. Later in the day another Catalina appeared and dropped a radio transmitting set by parachute. Although the set struck the water with a "resounding thump", it worked and, to the astonishment of the sailors, worked mechanically. "You turned a crank handle until a light glowed and that showed that the S O S was automatically being transmitted," was how Captain Matthews described this new wonder.

Just before dusk, the Catalina was over the boats again. She signalled "Good-bye, good luck," as a "Good night" message. But the forlorn men in the boats, according to their own accounts, thought "So what?" as they munched a biscuit and a piece of pemmican each and shared a dipper of water.

"And so, after setting watches, to bed—bolt upright in almost every case," wrote Captain Matthews. "The night seemed bitterly cold but as most of the Lascars had got away in only their 'lungies', it was agreed that they had first claim on the blankets. Officers and gunners made do with the weather

"Clan Campbell" and U.S.S. "Rhona"

"The Clan ship had the unusual
distinction of being ordered to stand
by the sinking merchantman"

clothes we had taken from the rafts. It was a very uncomfortable night as the boats rolled heavily and sea-anchors proved useless. To make things still more uncomfortable, three whales in sportive mood circled round us for most of the night, so close at times that when they "blew" to windward, the vapour descended on us and stank most foully. We had previously made the boats fast to each other, but quickly let go, lest the whales fouled the painters. A cold dawn with heavy rain, which thoroughly soaked everyone, did not cheer us any. But wet and miserable as we were, we did not neglect to keep our eyes lifted for a possible Catalina. No luck, so we transmitted again every half-hour."

The end of this brief epic came when Apprentice Lindsay—half-way up the mast because smoke had been seen on the horizon—verified that a ship was coming towards them. It was a French sloop, which gave the survivors a few more despondent minutes when, in the course of zig-zagging, she turned right away from them. Another alteration of course brought her quickly among the boats. As soon as the survivors had been picked up she was away again at full speed without even stopping to sink the empty boats.

"We were picked up at 8 a.m. on Friday the 13th—the sailor's unlucky day," wrote Captain Matthews, rounding off his graphic account with a large-sized query.

Chapter Nine

The Mediterranean Highway Again

Without your devoted service, there could be no
victory for our armies. From the Master in command, to
the boy on his first voyage, you have worked together with
the steady discipline of free men who know what is at stake.
Your reward is the consciousness of duty done and the
affection and respect of all your countrymen.

H.M. The King's Message, Christmas, 1943

WE HAVE DWELT UPON THE UNTIMELY END OF FINE SHIPS AND
have seen at the moment of their passing fresh evidence of
the unbroken courage of the men who served in them. From
the Master, with lifelong experience, to the youngest Apprentice, from "the Chief" to the soft-spoken Indian Fireman,
there came contributions to the apparently inexhaustible pool
of human courage.

After four years of war, these men sailing under the Red
Ensign were still prepared to make further contributions, and
they had not the satisfaction of knowing, as we know now,
that the worst of their ordeal was over. Indeed, in the six
months that we review in this chapter, only one ship of the
merchant fleets we are dealing with was sunk. The fifth year
of the war was only five days old when Italy surrendered
unconditionally and, although this did not mean that the
Mediterranean had been entirely cleared of the enemy, it
very materially altered the situation in that sea.

Clan ships had sailed in the Mediterranean in the days when Malta was earning its George Cross, and now they were to sail there again with increasing freedom. Masters of British ships found little to be jubilant about in the Italian surrender. It was just one of the stages on the road to final Victory. Their calm faith was reflected in the passing comment of Captain Booth when, from the bridge of the S.S. *Lieut. St. Loubert Bie*, he watched surrendering units of the Italian Navy sail into Alexandria. "Had a very good view of the Italian Fleet when they sailed in here, and all looked in very good condition," he recorded, in two lines.

But if events in and around the Meditreranean meant, as many believed, that the writing was on the wall for the enemy as a whole, there was still much damage they could do before they were compelled to see it. German morale was bolstered with talk of secret weapons, and one of these, the acoustic torpedo, made its appearance in the Atlantic about this time.

The ship that was lost, the *Banffshire*, of the Houston Line, went down in the far away Indian Ocean. She was torpedoed at night and sank in twenty minutes, but, when survivors were mustered next morning, it was found that only one rating was missing. Her Master, Captain H. Evans, had been torpedoed in the same sea only thirteen months earlier—when in command of the *Harmonides*.

Among the many long voyages completed in the autumn of 1943 was that of the *Clan Macnair* (Captain T. A. Watkinson). She had been away since the first day of February and had known the usual long spells of uneventful but watchful sailing, interspersed with occasional unusual incidents. The first of the latter happened while the ship was riding out three gales in the Gourock anchorage in February. The temperature of the water at the time was only 34 degrees and the surprise of the Master and Chief Officer can be imagined

145

when they looked over the side one evening, after hearing faint cries for help, and saw a naked man supported by a life-belt. The man, who was attempting to tow his clothes behind him on two more lifebelts, was exhausted. It was a very dark night and the Aldis lamp had to be switched on before helpers in the *Clan Macnair* could see to get the swimmer out of the water. Pulled up on to the deck, his teeth chattered so much that he could not speak. He was given half-a-tumbler of whisky and wrapped in blankets and put to bed. His strange but true explanation next day was that he was cook in another ship in the anchorage and had tried to swim ashore to see the Shipping Master. He had served in the Commandos and it was there that he had learned the trick of towing his gear after him. He was returned to his own ship by a more orthodox route.

By mid-May, the *Clan Macnair* was sailing in convoy out of Lourenço Marques with one other British ship, two American vessels and one Norwegian and one Danish ship. When only twenty-five miles north-east of Cape St. Lucia, the *Macnair* had a narrow escape as two torpedoes passed very close to her and struck the other British ship. As far as the *Macnair* was concerned, although the greatest sympathy was felt for those in the other ship, a miss was as good as a mile and she continued her voyage to various Indian ports.

Fully loaded, she made a non-stop run to Alexandria through the Suez Canal and, on September 14, was ready to sail as Commodore's ship of a Mediterranean convoy. On the way to Malta, Captain Watkinson and his men also had the pleasure of seeing the main units of the surrendered Italian Navy, escorted by British battleships and other vessels, pass on their way to Alexandria. An idea of the activity going on in the Mediterranean at that period was given by Captain Watkinson when he recorded: "Off Malta, the Malta and

Sicily ships left us and others joined, and then all the way along the North African coast we were dropping ships and picking up others at the various ports we passed."

The convoy of thirty-six ships in which the *Macnair* sailed from Gibraltar on September 25, had an impressive escort. In addition to five destroyers and three corvettes, there was a cruiser and a monitor, the latter, no doubt, returning for future business nearer home. On October 1, there was a "Brock's benefit" when German aircraft flew over the convoy in cloudy weather. First the cruiser, out ahead of the convoy, put up a barrage with her long-range anti-aircraft guns, and then the destroyers, corvettes and merchant ships joined in. The enemy spent most of the time in the clouds, and although twelve bombs were seen to drop in the vicinity of the convoy, none did any damage.

The S.S. *Lieut. St. Loubert Bie*, already mentioned, came home shortly after the *Macnair*, her voyage, too, having lasted for about eight months. Her experiences had included heavy south-west monsoon weather and, later, blinding sand storms in the Gulf of Aden. These were insignificant incidents, however, in comparison with an unhappy event which marked the passage of the outward convoy to the Cape. An ammunition ship quite close to the *St. Loubert Bie*, was torpedoed and blew up. "My ship was literally lifted and then heeled over to port, putting the gunwale under water," Captain Booth wrote. Water and debris crashed down on the ship, both compasses were broken, the dynamo stopped and the wireless was put out of action. Much damage was done on deck but nobody was injured. Among the "few tons" of metal and debris collected later in the *St. Loubert Bie*, the crew found shells from the sea-bed, although the depth of water was much more than a mile.

The *Clan Forbes*, the ship whose fortunes we have followed

closely from the earliest days of the war, and the *Clan Macbean* both arrived home before the end of October, 1943, having sailed out together in a vast convoy of eighty-three ships early in May. The *Macbean*, senior in age by twenty years, had made a useful trip to Algiers (where Mr. Churchill put in one of his sudden appearances), and then down the west coast of Africa. Her much bigger and faster sister had gone to Mombasa, Diego Suarez and Tamatave and then across the Indian Ocean to Calcutta and Colombo. Captain Banbury, of the *Clan Forbes*, before writing: "This safely concludes Voyage 8," declared: "Enemy activity has been sufficiently near at most times during the voyage to render it unnecessary to guard against complacency. My anxieties have been brightened by a fine ship and an excellent staff of officers—navigating, engineer and radio—and a good ship's company generally."

For the *Macbean*, doing her steady eight knots, it was the completion of her fifty-ninth voyage. Although she would not seek comparison with her fine modern sister, the value of such long and consistent service cannot be over-estimated. Two men will remember the *Macbean* with gratitude on that particular trip, Captain Simpson giving passage to a Chief Officer and a Chief Steward who had been waiting for some months to get home from Lagos.

A similar comparison might be made between two other ships, the *Clan Macdonald* and the *Clan Macgillivray*, which arrived in the Mersey within a day or two of each other. It was the completion of the eighth voyage for the *Macdonald* and the sixty-fifth for the *Macgillivray*. The *Macdonald* had been to Sydney. Heavily laden with food, she had encountered very bad weather on the early part of the homeward voyage. Forced to heave-to for seven hours, Captain Parfitt said ruefully: "For the first time in fifteen months I had to send a message to the Admiralty saying I was a hundred miles behind.

I have had occasion to send several messages saying that I was a hundred miles in front."

The *Macgillivray's* voyage had been round the Cape to Colombo, and back through the Suez canal and the Mediterranean. Although she was outward-bound in home waters as early as the latter part of April, 1943, the improving situation was reflected in the words of her Master (Captain R. Douglas) when he said: "It was the best organised convoy I ever sailed in, both as regards quantity and quality of escort, air support, and the more direct route steered."

Two interesting calls were made by the *Macgillivray* on the way to the Cape. A big welcome was waiting for her when she arrived at the island outpost of Ascension. For six months, the small community on the island had been waiting for mail from home. Twice they had known that a ship was on the way and twice they had had the disappointment of hearing that their mail and their supplies had been lost at sea. Three days after this visit, the *Macillivray* was at the other famous "dot" on the maps of the South Atlantic, St. Helena. While the heavy swell which broke at the mole impeded the discharge of cargo from the Clan ship, Captain Douglas and his Chief Engineer, Mr. Black, were pleasantly entertained by H.E. the Governor, Major Bain-Grey, and his wife. The Merchant Navy Master did not disguise the satisfaction which an invitation to lunch at Government House gave him. Although he may not have anticipated being quoted, I feel that more good than harm will be done by recording Captain Douglas reference to this visit. "After an excellent lunch," he wrote, "the Governor informed us that his car was at our disposal and said we ought to visit Longwood and Napoleon's Tomb. His wife insisted that we should return for tea. It was a most delightful day, and my respect for representatives of the Crown went up enormously."

Although we must go back ten months in order to sail with her from the Clyde in early January, 1943, a round voyage with the *Clan Farquhar* provides an excellent example of conditions at sea generally during this crucial year. Within a day or two of leaving with a convoy arranged in a sailing order of eleven lines, the *Farquhar* ran into a succession of heavy gales accompanied by snow and hail. Fortunately there was no sign of the enemy, but avoiding action was taken when part of a landing-craft was mistaken for a submarine. The gunners in one of the escorting corvettes—surely the most remarkable bad weather ships of the whole war—sank the section with their second shot.

The *Farquhar* had a rear position in the convoy, and mountainous seas and poor visibility shut her off from the Commodore's ship. With all the cabins flooded and the deck cargo being badly buffeted, Captain A. G. Storkey was relieved when the rear starboard ship hove-to. He decided that the general order which he had been expecting had been given. Next morning, however, only four ships were in sight, and the Master of the *Clan Farquhar* hurried after the convoy, which he found had managed to push on another fifteen miles. Not all ships rejoined the main convoy.

That evening visibility was practically nil owing to blinding snow. For seven hours the Master did not stir from the bridge of the *Farquhar* and then, as soon as he had gone down for "a cup of tea in comfort", the unexpected—or expected—happened. A steamer on the port beam came out of a snow flurry, heading straight for the *Farquhar*. With every second counting, Mr. W. Graham (Second Officer) who was on watch, ordered the helm to be put hard-a-starboard, at the same time thumping with his foot on the deck over Captain Storkey's room. The Master was on the bridge again at once, but by the time he got there another unpleasant factor in the shape of a ship on the starboard side had complicated the situation. Second Officer Graham had already put the engine-room telegraphs at "Full Speed Astern" and there was nothing more that he and the Master could do, except pray that their ship would gather stern way quickly enough to avoid a collision. Other anxious eyes must have been looking out into that wild, bitter night because the steamer on the port side straightened up. The other vessel crossed the bows of the *Farquhar* but thanks to the prompt action of the Second Officer, there was still a narrow margin between the ships when her stern finally slipped by. The strain of such incidents may well be imagined when one considers that the cost of a moment's indecision could be the lives of scores of men.

Many good things have been said of the Commodores of Convoys, but there were occasions when Masters felt bound to criticise their work. The Master of the *Farquhar* had his own opinion of the way this outward-bound convoy was handled. "Ships in columns were keeping too far apart," he declared, "so we were more often made to overlap than keep in the convoy. The Commodore was in a ballasted tanker and, in my opinion, failed to appreciate the difficulties of heavy laden cargo vessels in heavy weather. Signalling was down to a minimum. On three occasions course was altered without any signal being seen by the rear ships."

On February 2, Chief Officer Simpson sighted a raft and the *Farquhar* circled it. There was no sign of life on it, but the open bread tank and a white cotton canvas dodger which was hoisted, left little doubt that somebody had been on it at one time.

From Pernambuco, the Clan ship went on to Walvis Bay where one of H.M. ships lying in the port signalled to Captain Storkey when he was still five miles away: "Please advise nature of your cargo and your speed." "This information, if required, could have been obtained at the Routeing Office," the Master commented, "and I must say I was astonished that, after three years of war, those in charge of one of His Majesty's ships could be so indiscreet as to expect me to flash this information so that anyone in the town could have read it."

Between Cape Town and Durban, Captain Storkey was himself Commodore of a convoy of fifteen ships, which was later joined by the *Clan Colquhoun*. The Master commended the "teamwork" of his convoy, which was given the finest air cover he had experienced during the war. Submarines were twice heard of, but happily not seen, before the *Farquhar* arrived in Colombo. Half an hour before the ship was due to sail from Colombo for Australian ports, a slight whisp of smoke was seen coming from one of the ventilators. It gave warning of fire and was the beginning of an anxious three days for everybody in the ship. Lloyds' Surveyor, who was called in, suggested the lower hold should be flooded, but Captain Storkey, anxious to preserve his cargo, disagreed. A good deal of cargo was discharged, but when, after thirty-six hours, some of the hatches were taken off, smoke-helmets had to be used. Steam was injected and, after another two days, all the heated coal, which had caused the trouble, was clear. Although a vast amount of work had been involved, neither ship nor cargo was damaged.

The *Farquhar* struck a bad patch between Fremantle and Sydney when she was carrying a 35-ton rescue launch and several 9-ton launches. A lieutenant and six ratings of the United States Navy had charge of the large launch. The trouble started when one of the smaller launches was hit by a heavy sea and broke its lashings. Captain Storkey went aft while it was being secured, and had a narrow escape from being washed overboard by a sea which struck him in the back. The mass of water pushed him against the hatchway and he suffered nothing worse than a bruised shoulder and ankle and a thorough soaking. During the day, the weather got worse and it was impossible to continue on a zig-zag course, although the ship was in a recognised submarine area. The American naval Lieutenant was with the Master when, at 7.30 p.m., two enormous seas came over the bows almost together and struck the 35-ton launch with such force that it sounded like a clap of thunder. As they rushed out to see what had happened, the Master exclaimed: "Your launch has gone," and the Lieutenant, no more optimistic, said: "That's it." But the launch had not gone, although the heavy chocks under the bow and stern had been washed away. There were two individuals even more certain of disaster than Captain Storkey and the Lieutenant. They were two of the ratings who, with commendable courage, had decided to hide their lack of sea legs from the British by remaining in the launch. They were on their way aft when the Chief Officer met them. They stopped only to say: "We do not know what has happened but we have abandoned ship, sir!"

Exactly six months after sailing from Britain, the *Clan Farquhar* arrived in New Zealand. On the way from Auckland to Wellington she made herself useful as a "target" for torpedo-carrying planes of the New Zealand Air Force. Captain Storkey commented particularly on the warmth of the welcome extended to his officers and men by more than one New Zealand town.

Then the long run home by way of Balboa, Cristobel and New York, with a probable U-boat "kill" by one of the escort while crossing the Atlantic. And when the *Farquhar* came in she not only had her holds full of food and other valuable stores but her decks, too, were loaded with the sinews of war in the shape of aeroplanes and armoured vehicles.

The next voyage of the *Clan Farquhar*, which was much shorter, can be linked up with this story because she had completed another crossing of the Atlantic before the New Year was a fortnight old. Sailing again after only three weeks in the Clyde, the *Farquhar* was in St. John, New Brunswick, for Christmas. The weather was exceptionally cold, on one occasion reaching eighteen degrees below zero. Captain Storkey bought additional heating equipment for the crew's quarters but could do nothing about warming the hands of his officers who had much signalling to do when the Master of the *Farquhar* was chosen Commodore of the Halifax, St. John and North American ports section of the convoy. Most of the signals were made in answer to American ships, and Captain Storkey had some caustic comment to make on the volubility of American Masters. "As many as five ships were calling us up at the same time," he said, "and our lamp batteries were having to be charged twice a day to keep pace with them." Captain Storkey did not trust himself to enlarge on one particular ship which had left port without any charts and was constantly asking the way!

To pick up the threads of the autumn and winter story of 1943–44, the *Clan Macbrayne* had a fighting trip in convoy through the Mediterranean towards the end of October. Firstly, submarines were contacted and the *Macbrayne*, as leading ship on the port outer column, sighted a periscope at a distance of only six cables, and, secondly, determined air attacks developed. One attack by twenty-four planes lasted for an hour. A smoke-screen was put up to cover the convoy and both escorts and merchant ships let fly through it with their guns. "We had four attacks along our port side, and tracers from our oerlikon guns appeared to be hitting the after end of one plane," Captain Buckley stated later.

Two broadcasts picked up in the next few hours must have

given satisfaction to those in the convoy ships. From Marseilles there came an S O S for German airmen in distress eighteen miles north of where the attack took place, and then the B.B.C., who apparently knew more of what had happened than the men who had taken part in the action, announced that four planes had been shot down during an attack on a convoy off North Africa.

When the *Clan Colquhoun* arrived home after a voyage which had lasted just over twelve months, the Master, Captain Hogg, told of a terrific storm which his ship had encountered when about 200 miles off Mauritius. For hours, with the vessel hove-to, the wind was at hurricane force with frequent fierce rain squalls and visibility nil. Then the wind suddenly dropped and for about an hour there was a lull. After that the wind, which had changed direction completely, gradually grew in force until it was blowing a hurricane again. During the height of the storm, three lifeboats and two rafts were lost and two other lifeboats and a raft damaged.

"The loss of the boats was serious as we had 200 people on board at the time," Captain Hogg wrote. "There were only two boats left in davits in a seaworthy condition, and one small boat on No. 6 hatch. The total capacity of these three boats was seventy persons, and I therefore decided to put in to Port Louis." Of two boats Captain Hogg was successful in obtaining on loan there, one was the famous Trevessa lifeboat from the Naval Museum.

What the re-opening of the Mediterranean meant to British shipping in mileage alone it is almost impossible to estimate. Equally important was the saving of time, and Captain Townrow, bringing the *Buteshire* home from Calcutta by way of Suez, made the interesting note that he had accomplished in fifty days what it had taken 115 days to do on the previous voyage by the Cape route. The Germans tried hard to maintain a force of U-boats in the Mediterranean strong enough, at least, to harass our shipping. In November, 1943, it was estimated that there were twelve to fifteen German submarines in the Mediterranean, but they were having a very difficult time, and four U-boats were sunk when the enemy tried to reinforce them. A U-boat which carried out a successful attack was counter-attacked for more than thirty hours and then destroyed. In all seas, no less than fifty-three U-boats were sunk in the last quarter of 1943.

On very infrequent occasions there were odd occurrences that suggested that the enemy was still trying to achieve his ends by less straightforward ways than fighting. The *Clan Cameron* provided an example during a voyage which ended just before Christmas. The word "sabotage" was not used until a serious happening in the ship at Marmagoa, Portuguese West India. It was found that the port steering engine had been badly damaged, although strong anti-sabotage watches had been organised in the *Cameron*. The Master (Captain B. A. Hardinge) had laid down very definite instructions regarding the watches, and had arranged that his ship should be eight feet away from the quay so that no unauthorised person could get on board except by the gangways. The vessel was flood-lit as far as possible during the hours of darkness. Orders signed by the Master further laid it down that: "Men wearing 'Merchant Navy' badges are not to be allowed on board the vessel unless they are identified as friends of people on board. (I am assured that German sailors, speaking perfect English, have tried this dodge.) Box wallahs and bum-boat merchants are not to be allowed to board."

Captain Hardinge took the *Clan Cameron* back to Bombay for repairs, and all the facts were reported to the naval authorities. There had been two other mysterious happenings which, once the suspicion of sabotage was aroused, came into the picture. As the *Cameron* was about to pick up the pilot for Marmagoa, the port engine-room telegraph jammed. On investigation, after the ship had docked, a large piece of cotton-waste was found jammed at the first set of pulleys. After leaving port, the Sixth Engineer found a shell-fuse in a damaged ballast-pump casing which was standing on deck.

These matters naturally called for a careful inquiry on the part of the naval and civil authorities. The Master and a number of officers and men from the crew of the *Cameron* were required to give evidence before a Naval Board of Inquiry presided over by an Engineer-Commander. After five days, their considered opinion was that the damage had been caused by "negligence" and not sabotage, and there the matter had to rest.

More than one hundred American troops owed their lives to the valiant work of officers and men of the *Clan Campbell* after one of the last sinkings of 1943 in the Mediterranean. They were passengers in the S.S. *Rhona*, one of a number of troop transports that arrived in the Mediterranean towards the end of November. The *Clan Campbell* was in the convoy, which was attacked from the air as the light began to fade early one evening. The *Rhona* was set on fire by a direct hit and the Clan ship had the unusual distinction of being ordered by the Senior Officer of the Escort to stand-by the sinking merchantman. Captain H. M. Rodger at once took his ship as close to the *Rhona* as he dare and began to pick up survivors. When it was practically dark, two enemy planes flew over the burning ship and the *Campbell*, but fortunately no further attack developed.

The *Rhona* sank at 6.45 p.m. and the *Clan Campbell* was left alone, with a grim night's work ahead for her crew. Indians to the number of thirty-seven were picked up from one lifeboat, and then a second lifeboat was got alongside with a number of soldiers in it. It was found that a large proportion of them were suffering from fractured arms or legs and this made their rescue doubly difficult. Fortunately, two U.S. Army Air Force surgeons were among the uninjured and they attended to their less fortunate comrades. Captain Rodger got his 7,250-ton ship alongside another lifeboat which was waterlogged. Then, tragically, the men in it, seeing safety so close at hand, all scrambled at once towards the nets that had been let down over the side of the *Campbell*. The inevitable result was that the boat capsized and some men were lost and others were crushed by the heavy boat as it bumped against the merchant vessel. Seaman Gunner McNeil, and several of his shipmates in the *Clan Campbell*, went down the nets in the darkness to help exhausted survivors to climb on board.

More survivors were on rafts or in the water and the rescue work went on for hour after hour by the "spotlight" of an Aldis lamp. Some of the rafts had glimmering lights, but others could only be located by the whistles or shouts of those on them. "A ship of this size is not very suitable for rescue work, particularly at night," Captain Rodger wrote regretfully in his report. "Manœuvring to get alongside rafts is necessarily a slow business. The height of the deck from the water is a further drawback as every man to be pulled up is a deadweight. It is suggested that soldiers, before embarkation, should be instructed how to place themselves in a bowline. Taking a turn or two round the wrist and being pulled up a ship's side in that way is likely to be hurtful."

Five hours after the *Rhona* sank, the *Clan Campbell* came to the end of her heroic rescue work and headed for Phillipville with a total of 149 survivors on board. Three days later, she rejoined the convoy.

Three ships belonging to the associated fleets, the *Lanarkshire* and *Berwickshire* (of the Scottish Shire Line) and the *Clan Macneil*, arrived in the Mersey on the same day, February 23, 1944. Perhaps the Masters and crews got together at some time and talked over their varied experiences. They would have had plenty to talk about, but here we must skim lightly over months of arduous sailing that had taken them to many parts of the world. The *Lanarkshire*, in eight months, had been to Australia, back to Port Said and then out to Australia again. There was still much enemy submarine activity in the waters she had traversed, and Captain O'Byrne's story would have been one of almost ceaseless vigil. The great Captain Cook himself would have followed his courses with interest, taking in as they did such out-of-the-way ocean landmarks as Lord Howe Island, Norfolk Island, Pitcairn and Easter Islands, Chatham Islands and the southern coast of New Zealand and Tasmania. Once, the experienced British Master told the United States Naval Control that the route given him was not suitable for a vessel of light draught in winter, but when he was told that the orders came from the naval authorities in Washington and could not be altered, he made no further demur.

Captain Lynch, of the *Clan Macneil*, would have told how, when a few days out from Colombo and sailing alone, he had exchanged the "time of day" with two corvettes, and had then been invited to join their company. He would no doubt have said, as he wrote in his report: "Sailing with them all the way to Aden, I wondered if a cargo of ground nuts had ever before been carried across the Arabian Sea under such close convoy!" Finally, he would have mentioned the run home with no less than eighty-five vessels in convoy, including sixteen large landing-craft.

For the *Berwickshire*, Captain Inman would have recalled

going out with a convoy of equal size. He, too, had made friends with a British destroyer and had had her as escort for the last forty-eight hours before reaching Colombo. The weather, as must always be the case, would have come into the reminiscences of these sailormen, and the Master of the *Berwickshire* would have recalled how he very nearly succeeded in keeping clear of a cyclone which he "got the smell of" on the way back from Australia. On the fringe of it, his ship had taken one sea which carried away the after stanchions of the 4-inch gun platform.

It is fascinating to think of the stories that might have been exchanged even among the Masters coming back to this country around the time the three ships just mentioned arrived. Captain Campbell, of the *Empire Wisdom*, would have capped all the "ships in company" anecdotes by his account of a voyage from Cape Town to Durban with the battleship *Ramillies*, escorted by four destroyers and day and night air cover. Captain Woodriffe would have recalled how the *Clan Murdoch*, and the convoy she was with, had been pestered with U-boats for three days and four nights when they sailed nearly a year earlier. And he would not have forgotten that, according to the Vice-Commodore, three U-boats were sunk in less than eighteen hours. Captain McPherson would have told of a grandstand view of an aerial battle over the Mediterranean from the bridge of the *Clan Murray*, with unpleasant glider bombs distracting the attention from the much more pleasant business of watching Junkers shot into the sea. Captain Cater might have contented himself with a description of his homeward "cargo" of 28-ton tanks and 15-inch naval shells in the *Clan Ranald*, and Captain Pengelly could have rounded off a most interesting session with the story of how a memorable convoy of ninety-five ships, including the *Empire Forest*, was slowed down just as three large German ships, actually flying the swastika flag, left Oran with repatriated German prisoners. To the nationals of that country, who have never really understood the immense ramifications of the term "sea power", it must have been an almost incredible sight.

Chapter Ten

Behind the Great Assault

When I look back upon the fifty-five months of this
hard and obstinate war, which makes ever more exacting
demands upon our life-springs of energy and contrivance,
I still rate highest among the dangers we have overcome
the U-boat attacks upon our shipping, without which we
cannot live or even receive the help which our Dominions
and our grand and generous American ally have sent us.
WINSTON CHURCHILL, BROADCAST, MARCH 1944

AS THE DAYS LENGTHENED INTO THE SPRING of 1944, THE IM-
patient public demand for the opening of "the Second Front"
grew apace. There were some who believed that it would never
happen and that the war would be won by methods other than
direct assault. Even with Italy out of the war, we still had
armies to maintain in the Mediterranean zone. Offensively,
the R.A.F. and U.S. Air Forces were battering Germany almost
beyond human endurance, but a hard and stubborn enemy still
held on, and there was an uneasy feeling growing among our
own people that there might be more behind the "secret
weapons" claim of Hitler than we had at first given him credit
for.

The Services were just as anxious for the opening of the
Second Front as the chalk-and-whitewash gentlemen who
wrote their appeals on inviting stretches of wall or hoarding.
For many months I had had the opportunity of seeing soldiers,

sailors and, less frequently, airmen preparing for the Great Day. Only a few weeks before it dawned, some tough Canadian troops confided to me their anxiety lest the war should be over before they had the chance to play the part for which they had so strenuously prepared.

Such glory as there is in war—and we know now, for the second time in a generation or two, that modern war is exhausting and destructive for both victor and vanquished—comes chiefly in victory. There are few to-day, for instance, who remember the inspired courage of the late Lord Gort's decision to bring his small and shattered army to the beaches of Dunkirk, when he might have thrown all responsibility for even greater disaster on the shoulders of the War Cabinet, by accepting the advice conveyed to him to fight his way through to rejoin the French. Nor is the retreat through Burma held by the public in such esteem as some subsequent minor victories. It is fair, therefore, that before dealing with the events of June, 1944, as they concern this narrative, one's personal conviction should be set down: that the greater share of credit for victory is due to those who achieved, so much sometimes even in defeat, *before* we crossed the Normandy beaches.

We have used the term "glory in war" in its widest sense. That it can be used on a different plane is amply proved by the stories already told in this book. Perhaps the only real compensation offered to humanity by war is to be found in the endurance and courage it engenders in individuals. In the immortal words of Rupert Brooke:

> "Honour has come back, as a king, to earth,
> And paid his subjects with a royal wage;
> And Nobleness walks in our ways again;
> And we have come into our heritage."

And the sad thought is that when peace comes there is so

often a return to pettiness when we fall from these high, un-selfish standards.

The ships that had maintained the lifeline of this country from September, 1939, onwards were as vital to the eventual mounting of the great attack that was to take us back to Western Europe as were those that sailed in early 1944. In the last few months before the Allied armies sailed to the initial assault there were direct indications that more and more ships were being used for the pre-Invasion build-up. While food and other necessary supplies continued to come from Australia, New Zealand, India, South Africa and South America, even more significant cargoes were being loaded in crowded ports along the North American seaboard. Big ships made speedy westward crossings of the North Atlantic in ballast, to load the latest weapons of war, and in every fast convoy returning there were thousands of American troops. One fast convoy that I sailed with from New York was typical of the impressive strength that the great Republic was pouring into the battle outpost of Britain. It included four heavily-laden troopships (in fine weather, men appeared like ants on their decks), a United States battleship, two American-built aircraft carriers, with their flight-decks covered with American-type Fleet Air Arm fighters, and eleven U.S.N. destroyers as escort.

Powerful United States naval forces were functioning both ways, and the T.S.S. *Empire Wisdom* (operated by the Clan Line) sailed in ballast for New York in February in company with the U.S. battleship *Nevada* and an escort of twelve American destroyers. She returned in a convoy of twenty-seven ships, mostly tankers flying the Stars and Stripes, and with six U.S. destroyers in attendance. The speed of the convoy was fifteen knots, an increase over the old six and eight-knot convoys which more than discounted the improved speed of the new U-boats. Her full cargo included amphibious tanks, cased aircraft and two winches of twenty-five tons each.

The *Clan Farquhar* also crossed to New York in ballast, with a convoy of over fifty ships. There was one noisy night with "star shells being sent up all round the compass and depth charges being dropped at frequent intervals." The day that followed was quiet but, judging by previous experience, Captain Storkey and his men were ready for further trouble when darkness came. Instead, with reinforcements arriving for the already strong escort, the U-boats broke off the action. There was another incident of a more domestic nature in the *Farquhar* during a dense fog. It can be readily pictured from the Master's own short account: "During the fog on the morning of February 25, the seacunny appeared to be very excited in the wheelhouse. The Second Officer and I looked in to see what was the matter—and there was the seacunny with the wheel in his hands completely clear of the steering gear, and looking like a naughty child. The Second Officer had the wheel on again in a few seconds, the key having worked loose on the spindle. . . ."

Among the ships coming from further afield were the *Clans Macdonald* and *Urquhart* from South America, the *Perthshire* from Australia and the *Clan Matheson* from India. The *Urquhart* had made a fast run after setting out with a fourteen-knot convoy, and the *Macdonald* put in a claim to the war-time record for a cargo vessel on the round trip between this country and Buenos Aires. Actually, the record was claimed for the previous voyage of the *Macdonald* when she was out and back in fifty-six days. The Master (Captain Parfitt) was satisfied that he could have improved on the time on his last voyage, but for drastic changes of route which had to be made on instructions from the naval authorities. He had good grounds for his belief, his outward passage time from the Bar Light Vessel to the Recalada

Light Vessel being only eighteen days and forty-five minutes. The sailing distance was 7,006 miles.

Although she had called at Fremantle, Adelaide, Melbourne, Gladstone, Brisbane and Sydney, the *Perthshire*, with Captain W. R. Roberts in command, had only been away for a little over four months. Leaving the Clyde one week before Christmas, 1943, she was in Fremantle by January 23, 1944. It was not until she was on the last hundred miles of her homeward run that the *Perthshire* saw signs of enemy activity. Then, fortunately, it was only an aircraft dropping flares which lit up the whole sea but did not produce any offensive action.

Of the four "long distance ships" coming home practically together, the *Clan Matheson* had been away for by far the longest time. She had gone down Thames from the London docks on April 24, 1943, and, as a start to thirteen months of almost continuous sailing, had encountered icebergs and fog on the way to New York. From the United States, she had taken a cargo to South African ports, calling at Trinidad on the way. Then the *Matheson* had worked her way up to the Persian Gulf, and, after an exchange of cargo, on to the Indian ports. Following a trip to Colombo, she was back in Calcutta by the end of November and then, on December 5, suffered a direct hit from a Japanese bomber. Five labourers were killed and a fire was started in the ship. While this was being fought by the crew of the *Matheson*, another wave of Japanese aircraft appeared. Bombs hit the quay and were close enough for some of the splinters to cut the stern moorings of the Clan ship. Despite the distractions, the officers and men of the *Matheson* quickly had the fire out and, as Captain Arthur MacIntyre, her Master, observed, their courage probably saved a very damaging fire from taking hold, as a large amount of jute was in the open holds. The bomb damage repairs caused a short break in the sea-time of the *Matheson*, but she sailed fully laden for home in February, 1944, and using the Mediterranean route, went non-stop past Gibraltar, her onward sailing instructions being passed to her at sea by one of H.M. ships.

The supply columns of the United States Army were directly maintained by Clan ships that had been in the front line for most of the war. The *Clan Colquhoun* went in ballast to New York and returned with about half of her 6,400 tons of cargo in the form of hard frozen meats for American troops. Through the Trade Division of the Admiralty, the Master, Captain A. J. Hogg, received this commendation from the Commodore of the outward convoy: "*Clan Colquhoun* was particularly good at station-keeping, signalling and in passing me frequent observed positions." It was a Red Ensign Commodore who paid the compliment—Commodore H. J. Anchor, O.B.E., R.D., R.N.R. Weather on the return passage made up for fair conditions on the westbound crossing. In a westerly gale which lasted for four days, heavy seas broke down doors and flooded all cabins. Many of the cabins were not habitable for over a week.

The *Lanarkshire*, proceeding independently, also experienced some of this bad weather on her way to New York. Although speed was her chief safeguard, Captain O'Byrne was compelled to slow down because his big ship was "rolling, pitching, straining heavily and, at times, pounding". The convoy with which the *Lanarkshire* returned had an escort of one cruiser and twelve destroyers, all of the United States Navy, and a speed of thirteen-and-a-half knots was maintained all the way. The destroyers were not slow to use their depth charges. Attacks went on from early morning until late in the evening one day. "From what I could hear on the radio telephone later, fish were the cause of the frequent attacks on this day," Captain O'Byrne dryly commented. But even the Chief Engineer, whose department suffered most, was prepared to agree that the disturbance caused by the depth-charging of shoals of fish was preferable to the presence of "tin fish" among the ships of the convoy.

As a relief to the grim concentration behind the fast-approaching Second Front, the *Clan Macbean*, 5,000-ton veteran, came home with a new kind of *Arabian Nights'* story. Her adventures were concerned with two barges which, at the request of the Ministry of War Transport, she attempted to tow from Abadan to Karachi. But the spell of the Arabian Sea must have been upon those two inanimate craft because, after a quiet start, they quickly became the elusive centre of much activity.

The *Macbean* had proceeded a little more than 100 miles on her way when, in the small hours of the morning, the tow-rope, which Captain Simpson was careful to point out was supplied by the Ministry of War Transport, decided to part. The Clan ship, free of her encumbrances, immediately picked up a knot or two, but two barges, especially when consigned by the Ministry of War Transport, are not to be shaken off as easily as that. Nobody knew that better than Captain Simpson, so he curbed the impatience of his ship (an impatience which in due course was to be shared by most of his officers and crew) and came around and stopped in the vicinity of the barges. Now the weather during the night had been fine, but even in the few hours that remained before daylight what most sailors would have regarded as a "safe bet" happened— the weather started to deteriorate. It was impossible to board the barges, so the first mild radio message went off to the N.C.S.O., Abadan: "Tow-rope parted near barge in position ——. Please send tug and another tow-rope. Am standing by."

The *Macbean* was left contemplating the two forlorn barges and the end of the broken tow-rope. There was plenty of time to see that the tow-rope was stranded for its whole length and was unfit for further use before a polite reminder was des-

168

patched at 10.45 a.m.: "Weather conditions still deteriorating. Awaiting reply to my first message."

Two hours later the reply came: "No tug available. If both barges adrift, continue to stand-by. If one is still in tow, proceed to Bandar Abbas. Report your position." Those in the tossing *Macbean* must have looked longingly at each barge in turn, but the fact remained that both were adrift and Captain Simpson hastened to add that to the earlier information supplied. He also mentioned that the barges were still connected together and that a heavy sea was running.

By 4 p.m., more than twelve hours after the tow-rope had parted, a slight impatience was to be discerned in another follow-up message sent out from the *Macbean*: "Cannot stand-by indefinitely under present weather conditions. No men on barges. Request permission to proceed Bandar Abbas. Reply immediately."

A little over five hours later, the *Macbean* picked up the reply: "Am sending an armed whaler to stand-by barges. On her arrival you may proceed to Bandar Abbas for orders, but if weather moderates before her arrival, endeavour to resume tow." This was followed, at fifteen minutes past midnight, with the following: "Important. Whaler proceeding to your assistance. Report your position every six hours."

From that time, it became a one-sided "conversation". The *Macbean* gave her position and added: "Thick sand haze. Endeavouring to keep contact with barges. Strong N.W. wind. Drift now S.E." At 2 a.m. she passed the information: "Regret contact with barges lost, but remaining in the vicinity. Hope to regain contact when visibility improves." This was followed at 6.55 a.m. with: "Position ———. Steering 171 degrees. Speed four knots. Searching for barges. When last seen, bumping heavily together." The anxiety expressed in the last sentence was relieved soon afterwards and, at 7.20 a.m.,

Captain Simpson signalled: "Contacted barges position ——.
Standing by again."

After another five-and-a-half watchful hours, the armed
whaler arrived. On instructions, the merchantman made a
lee for the whaler so that some of her crew could attempt to
board the leading barge. At 2 p.m. the Clan ship was told to
stand-by again, as the swell was too heavy for the men to
transfer from the whaler to the barge. A quiet half-hour
went by and then the whaler signalled the *Macbean*: "Proceed
Bandar Abbas for orders and leave barges in my charge."
The *Macbean* proceeded at full speed.

To come nearer home again in the month or two that remained before the Allied armada arrived in the Bay of the
Seine, activity at sea was reaching its climax. The enemy, who
had been able to sink only one ship in convoy in the North
Atlantic throughout the month of March, could do little to
halt the build-up. Fewer U-boats were operating because the
"Schnorkel", which was to enable submarines to remain submerged for much longer periods, was about to make its
appearance. Nevertheless, with new hunting devices, we sank
seventeen U-boats in the month of April, 1944.

A German Admiral has since declared that the loss of the
Mediterranean was the turning-point of the war for the Axis
powers. In a most lucid exposition written while he was a
prisoner-of-war, Vice-Admiral Weichold, who was Flag
Officer, German Naval Command, Italy, 1940–43, not only
made this statement shortly after the end of the war, but
accused the German High Command of lacking "sea sense".
"Without its Mediterranean positions secured," he wrote,
"the British Command would not have had the freedom of
movement in its rear, and the forces to spare to carry out a
landing in France. The importance of this position, and the
effect it could have on the whole war, was not recognised by

the German Command, although there was no lack of representations and warnings on this matter. The blame for the under-valuation of the fundamental naval character of this war must be carried not only by the highest political leaders, but also by the Supreme Command of the Armed Forces."

The *Empire Barrie*, the *Buteshire* and the *Commandant Dorise* were among the ships that used the broad highway of the Mediterranean to bring supplies to England in time for the invasion. More than 3,000 tons of copper, delivered to the Tyne, was included in the cargo of the *Empire Barrie*. The *Commandant Dorise* also had 2,500 tons of copper in a valuable mixed cargo, and the *Buteshire's* contribution included sisal, coffee, tea, kapok, beeswax and palm kernels. The changed times were especially reflected in the report of the Master of the *Commandant Dorise*, Captain Stone: "The passage through the Mediterranean and from Gibraltar to London was without incident."

A small "family party" had developed at one period of the *Buteshire's* long voyage. It was at Aden and on the subsequent passage to Mombasa. When the Convoy Conference was called, Captain Woodall, of the *Buteshire*, found that his Commodore was to be Captain Douglas, of the *Clan Macgillivray*, while the Senior Officer of the Escort was Lieutenant-Commander Thornton, D.S.C., R.N.R., who had been a Chief Officer in the Clan Line at the outbreak of war.

The irrepressible Captain Parfitt was making one more fast run in the *Clan Macdonald* before D-Day. He found exhilaration rather than strain in these expectant days, and was intrigued rather than disconcerted by the number of diversion instructions sent to him by the Admiralty on his way to and from Buenos Aires. A diversion brought him within sight of a convoy off the Azores. One of the escort vessels with the convoy moved to intercept the single ship, but Captain Parfitt, like the child of the prophet accepting the advice of Elisha, girded up his loins and ran. He did this so effectively that, in his own words, "it was funny because the escort ship could not catch me or get near me." Captain Parfitt, with a naïve pride in the performance of his ship, added: "I signalled him with the big lamp and gave my number and special signals. I received this message: 'Keep your course and speed and keep clear.' This was easy—I lost them in less than half-an-hour!"

As he neared home, Captain Parfitt recorded with typical zest and freshness: "At 8 p.m., May 13, sent a wireless message to the Admiralty informing them that I was 100 miles ahead of my position, allowing a speed of sixteen knots from Montevideo. At 9.30 a.m., May 16, received a very sharp diversion from London (ninety degree turn to the eastwards), and at 5 p.m. received another diversion from London. We are dodging something, and with this new diversion shall not lose much as we cut right into the North Channel with the next alteration, which will be in the morning." And, sure enough, all that remained to be said was: "Arrived safely at Liverpool and docked in the north-east Brocklebank Dock at 1.29 p.m., May 19."

Captain McCrone, who brought the *Berwickshire* into Liverpool on the same day with a big cargo of frozen foodstuffs for the United States Army which he had loaded in New York as recently as the first week in May, had experienced a "complete absence of the enemy above, on or below the water." His two worries had been the congested state of the docks in New York which had made him uneasy about the loading of his cargo, and fog, which had lasted for as much as fifteen hours on end during the homeward voyage.

Two more Clan ships, the *Macinnes* and the *Cameron*, beat D-Day by little more than hours. Both had stories to tell of the immense activity at sea which was the prelude to invasion.

The *Macinnes* had sailed for New York in convoy and had run into dense fog. Out of the fog, a Dutch steamer appeared for a few minutes and Captain Hinton Browne was surprised to receive a signal from her telling him to go to Quebec. The fog had swallowed her again before any return signal could be made. The Master of the *Macinnes* was mystified but decided that as the Dutchman knew the name of his ship, it was safe to accept the instructions. He was in the middle of the fog-bound convoy and it was only with difficulty that he got his ship clear and set course for the Gulf of St. Lawrence. That night there was a confirmatory radio message from the naval authorities at Halifax and also instructions for the *Macinnes* to rendezvous something—Captain Hinton Browne had no idea what—at a point already passed. That problem was solved by another message which gave him another rendezvous ahead of his position.

Ships were being sent to many unusual ports at this time and the *Macinnes* had sailed up the St. Lawrence through vast sheets of melting ice to Three Rivers, a town about sixty-five miles above Quebec. There she had discharged her sand ballast and had then proceeded to Montreal for loading. On the return voyage, fog, a fine cover against enemy observation, had cloaked the *Macinnes*, and the large convoy with which she sailed, for practically half the time. Congestion in ports on this side of the Atlantic led to another change of destination for the *Macinnes* during passage. She was directed to Belfast, sent on from there to Loch Ewe and finally arrived at Leith.

The *Clan Cameron*, coming home on the eve of D-Day after four months at sea, had sampled pre-invasion conditions both in the Mediterranean and the Atlantic. The outward voyage, with a full cargo of general merchandise and military stores, had taken her to Port Said. On the way, the convoy was attacked by seven enemy bombers, but the value of the escort carriers was proved when H.M.S. *Pursuer* sent her fighters into the air to shoot down two of the German planes and damage a third. From Port Said, the *Cameron* had carried another military cargo to Algiers and then, having been taken over by the Ministry of War Transport, she had sailed for New York. Like the *Macinnes*, her destination had been changed on the way, and she had found herself in Baltimore loading a cargo which included 2,000 tons of high explosives, 1,000 tons of slab and rod steel and a large consignment of foodstuffs.

The pressure on port organisations meant that Masters were often in difficulties while their ships were loading. Captain Hardinge, of the *Clan Cameron*, put his foot down when it was suggested that he should load without the 1,000 tons of steel. He pointed out that this must go in the bottom of the ship for stability reasons. He also decided that 25-ton tanks could hardly go on top of barrels of lard. There were other points of disagreement, but the experienced British Master stood firm on all matters that might affect the trim and stability of his ship.

If he was unimpressed with American port methods under the stress of unusual effort, Captain Hardinge was prepared to acknowledge the comforting strength of the United States Navy. As he sailed home across the Atlantic with a great convoy of ninety ships, he wrote: "I am impressed by the contrast between the escort provided for American convoys as compared with British. In the convoy from Algiers to U.S.A. with seventy vessels, we had over eighteen destroyers with an escort for each column, beam and stern escorts and a double screen ten miles outside. With this convoy of ninety ships we have seven miserable corvettes." The comment was no doubt justified, although the long and gallant record of service of the little corvettes had earned for them many descriptions other than "miserable". No reflection on the capacity of these hardy little ships as guardians was intended, as Captain Hardinge's final

"The destroyers were
not slow to use their
depth charges."

note made clear. "The whole convoy arrived without incident," he wrote.

So we come to that day, June 6, 1944, when, to quote a great Canadian, there was to be unfolded a story "of skill and forethought, devotion, resolution, preparedness, courage and overwhelming might unequalled in the annals of warfare." And in all these things the British Merchant Navy had its share. It also had the proud knowledge that without its dogged grit in the years of adversity, June 6, 1944, would never have dawned as the Day of Liberation for millions of men, women and children. As the landing-craft and other vessels filled the swept channels between England and France, they sailed not only in the spirit of Nelson and of Drake, but under the lee of a vast and ghostly fleet flying the Red Ensign.

It was Admiral Creasy, Chief of Staff to Admiral Sir Bertram Ramsay, Allied Naval Commander-in-Chief for the Invasion, who said shortly before "Zero Hour": "What Philip of Spain tried to do and failed; what Napoleon wanted to do and could not; what Hitler never had the courage to try, we are about to do, and with God's grace we shall." These pious, prophetic and proud words undoubtedly included the inestimable contribution made to our sea power by the officers and men of the Merchant Navy.

Few merchant ships had the actual satisfaction of taking part directly in "Operation Neptune", but one Clan ship, the *Clan Lamont*, played a leading role. Put on "V" Articles, the *Lamont* had spent most of May carrying out pre-invasion exercises off the Isle of Wight. At the beginning of June, she went into Southampton and 1,400 officers and men of the Canadian Army, who were to take part in the initial assault, were embarked. She then went to a position off Spithead.

At 9.20 on the night of June 5, Captain A. Campbell, Master of the *Clan Lamont*, gave the order to weigh anchor. With ships of all types and sizes, she steamed through the hours of darkness towards the French coast. A wonderful piece of internal organisation enabled all the soldiers to be served with a good breakfast at 4 a.m., and the *Lamont* anchored in her allotted position in the Bay of the Seine at 6.15 a.m.

Five minutes later, the troops in the first wave of the assault were heading towards the shore in their flat-bottomed boats. They had a great send-off it is said, because Captain Campbell, with the fighting blood of a famous line of Scots in his veins, had gone in with a piper on the bridge of his ship playing "The Campbells are coming!"

The *Clan Lamont* continued to carry troops between England and the Normandy bridge-head until July 2. In five crossings, she made the splendid contribution of 8,218 officers and men safely conveyed. Among the operational beaches she visited were Juno, Omaha and Utah. In his subsequent report Captain Campbell said: "The ship's company behaved excellently and I cannot speak too highly of the conduct of the Marines. . . . For the first time I realised the full meaning of sea-power."

Also in the Invasion fleet under the Red Ensign there were, of course, the old ships that sailed across the Channel to "sit" on the bottom stem to stern near the shore and so provide a shelter for the hundreds of small craft. They had typical Merchant Navy names such as *Empire Moorhen*, *Empire Bunting*, *Mariposa*, *Bendoran* and *Empire Waterhen* and, rusty and oil-covered as they soon became, they still retained their dignity. It was in the shelter of these old warriors that the King transferred from a powerful motor boat to the amphibious vehicle that carried him up the Normandy beaches on D-plus 10. My own home for nearly a fortnight after D-Day was H.M.S. *Hilary*, a converted banana vessel, that was headquarters-ship for Admiral G. N. Oliver.

Once the last great offensive of the war had started, supplies became an even more urgent matter than during the build-up period. The demand grew with our increasing commitments on the Continent. It was met by new ships as well as old. First vessel under the management of Cayzer, Irvine and Co. to arrive in Britain after the opening of the Second Front was the *Sambalt* (Ministry of War Transport owned) on her maiden voyage. American built, she had been launched on December 9, 1943, under the name *Robert Wycliffe*, but a British Master (Captain A. Hunter) and crew were waiting to take her over and she became the *Sambalt*. With 6,700 tons of cargo, she sailed from Brooklyn on January 19, and arrived at Abadan on March 11. She then carried a military cargo, including two 67-ton locomotives and their tenders on deck, to Port Said, and rounded off a maiden voyage of 18,236 miles by bringing a useful general cargo back to this country.

The *Empire Wisdom*, from Montreal, was several times diverted to avoid the heavy convoy traffic on the Atlantic. On her northerly route several icebergs were encountered, but Captain Cater brought her safely in to unload in the Royal Albert Dock, London, while our first reinforcements were still crossing to the Normandy beaches. A little later, the *Clan Campbell* arrived in Glasgow from the Cape. She was on time, although for several days she had been in a westerly gale. Captain Lofthouse told how the loading of his ship had been taken in hand at once as soon as she arrived at Cape Town, despite the fact that it was a public holiday.

As the D-Days turned into weeks, more ships were directed straight to London. Among them were the *Clan Macbrayne* from Madagascar, via the Cape, and the *Clan Farquhar* from Australian and New Zealand ports. In addition to her cargo of 900 tons of lead, 2,600 tons of dried fruit, 2,313 tons of frozen mutton and 800 hogsheads of tobacco, the *Farquhar* arrived with three stowaways who had got on board at an American port of call. They had appeared one after another over a period of thirty-six hours, and Captain Storkey must have wondered if his ship was carrying unofficial reinforcements for the American Army.

Another American-built ship, the *Samfield*, made her first appearance in a British port early in August. Under the command of Captain J. C. Scott, she had made two successful trips between the United States and Mediterranean ports.

With the fifth year of hostilities drawing to a close and the optimists saying: "All over by Christmas," there came a sad happening, the faithful old *Berwickshire*, of the Scottish Shire Line, being sunk by enemy torpedoes off the coast of South Africa. Her thirty years of service at sea, had included two wars, yet her Master, Captain J. McCrone, could write after watching his ship sink: "The *Berwickshire* herself took terrific punishment before she sank and stood up to it much longer than many a more modern vessel might have done. We watched the ship go with the greatest regret—and no one more so than myself."

The *Berwickshire* (7,464 tons) had sailed from Durban on her last voyage on the afternoon of August 18 as Commodore vessel of a small convoy bound for Tamatave and Mauritius. No naval staff was carried, Captain McCrone acting as Commodore. The six ships of the convoy were escorted by three small naval vessels, but soon after setting out one of these had to return to port with engine trouble. Three of the ships in the convoy proved to be so slow that it was eventually decided that the *Berwickshire* should proceed with the escort and two others at eight-and-a-half knots. It was in the early evening of the 20th, five minutes after an alteration of course, that the tanker *Daronia* was torpedoed. "Action stations" was sounded in the *Berwickshire* and the escort dropped depth charges. It was more than four hours later, when the suspense of Captain

McCrone and his men may well have been easing, that the U-boat struck again. Nothing had been seen of the submarine before the explosion amidships which smashed everything on the starboard side of the boat-deck. The main engines were put out of action, the steering gear and telegraphs rendered useless and the Chief Engineer, among others, found himself temporarily trapped in wreckage. The ship was in complete darkness. Third Engineer Brown, and Fourth Engineer Morrice who had gone below to keep his friend company although he knew the danger the ship was in, were both killed in the explosion.

"A second torpedo at any moment seemed a logical deduction," was the way Captain McCrone put it, and he was right. But before that came, he had got the surviving members of the crew away in two boats and on rafts. He was told on the bridge soon after the first explosion that three distress signals had been sent out on the emergency transmitter. The crew remained cool, although the Indians, having got into the boats, adopted a fatalistic attitude and could only with difficulty be persuaded to use the oars. None behaved with greater gallantry than Acting Petty Officer Ellery, who was in charge of the low angle gun's crew. He scrambled along the smashed boat-deck to tell one of the officers that he would remain with his gun as long as possible in the hope of "having a crack" at the submarine. Ellery was one of the last to leave the ship, himself slipping a raft at the last moment, from which he was picked up next morning.

Chief Officer Beynon and Third Officer Sintzenich were mentioned for the assistance they gave the Master at this time, as were Chief Engineer Spottiswood, who had to dig himself clear of the wreckage of his cabin, and Second Engineer Bowie. Apprentice Childs earned the commendation of the Master a little later. "He was in my boat and on leaving the ship's side he, in common with most of the others, was violently sick," Captain McCrone wrote. "In spite of this, he refused to leave an oar and pulled until he was completely exhausted."

As the two crowded boats pulled away, the second torpedo struck the *Berwickshire* and broke her back. She reared up like a great black "V" sign, and it was not until a third explosion, which may have been her own boilers blowing up in a final proud act of self-destruction, that the old ship sank. In the morning, when survivors were picked up by H.M.S. *Norwich City*, it was found that ninety-four were safe, and that eight of the crew—the Second Officer, the Senior Apprentice, two Watchkeeping and two Refrigerating Engineers, the Second Wireless Operator and one Indian greaser—had given their lives.

. . . . .

When September 3 came again to mark the start of the sixth and final year of the war, the *Clan Forbes*, on Voyage No. 10 of her career, was in waters not far removed from where the *Berwickshire* sank. Her previous voyage, completed nine weeks earlier, had taken her once again to India and Australia. Carrying a multitude of things, from green sand to filled mines and from grain to American Army stores, she had steamed 31,688 miles in little more than six months. With ever-present war risks adding to his normal burden of responsibility, the Master, Captain Andrews, apologised for the one mishap of a notable voyage, the sinking of a dhow that unwisely chose the deepwater channel as the big merchantman was leaving Bombay.

Chapter Eleven

Ships From Over the Sea

The Royal Navy and Merchant Navy services are equal
partners in a gigantic task which is now on the way to a
triumphant conclusion. The fight is now going to us, it is
now a winning battle, but we shall never forget the ordeals
of the Merchant Navy which have made these huge successes possible, and Britain must never forget either.

A. V. ALEXANDER,
FIRST LORD OF THE ADMIRALTY, JANUARY, 1945

THE RICHNESS OF BRITAIN'S ASSETS IN SHIPS AND THE MEN TO
man them has been fully demonstrated in these pages but, as
the drain of war continued, there were other assets on shore
relating to sea power that became increasingly important.
We had the men who could draw from a vast mine of experience when it came to operating fleets of ships; we had the
expert builders; we had the ship-repairers; and we had the
marine engineers. In one year alone (1942), 259 merchant
ships with a total tonnage of over 1,300,000 were built in
British yards, and enemy bombing and the black-out did not
prevent us from launching considerably more tonnage in the
four years 1940–43 than we did in the four years 1915–18.
Our yards had as much as 2,600,000 tons of shipping under
repair at one time.

From the start it was clear that all these "back room boys"
of the war at sea would have to work against time. It was
no use pointing to the difficulties left over from the days of

depression. Ships were needed as replacements, and the all-important thing was that those ships should go to work without loss of time. Thousands of men and women helped to put the whole machine behind the front-line sailor into top gear in an amazingly short space of time. It was an effort that still remained invaluable even when America began to mass-produce ships.

In the latter part of the war it was the contribution of tonnage from the other side of the Atlantic that rapidly became decisive. Before 1944, Mr. Churchill was able to say: "The output of new building from the United States has fulfilled all that was ever hoped from it, and more." The sinking of the *Berwickshire* in August, 1944, brought the total of losses of the Clan and associated fleets to thirty-five ships. Happily, many of the Masters, with experienced officers and men, had survived and were only too anxious to get to sea again. The organisation that had operated the fleets when they were at full strength still existed. It was the natural and sensible course that as new ships came into the Allied pool they should be manned by proved British crews and operated by those who, in peace and in war, were used to meeting—even anticipating —the needs of ships in all parts of the world.

Before the new ships appeared, Cayzer, Irvine and Co., from the London office shadowed by the church in narrow St. Mary Axe, from Glasgow and from Liverpool, were operating a number of ships, including some former French vessels, for the Ministry of War Transport. A proportion of them had taken the prefix Empire in place of the well-known Clan. In the latter months of the war, another prefix, never to be forgotten by those who saw the business through to its end at sea, was to come prominently into the record. The "Sams" appeared in ever-increasing numbers.

No less than twelve of these big Liberty ships—they were

all of over 7,000 tons gross—were operated by the Managers
of the Clan Line Steamers. One or two have already been
mentioned, but it was towards the end of 1944 that the full
flood of these ships came like a reviving blood transfusion into
the main supply arteries at sea. British Masters, used to well-
founded vessels and with a natural distrust of prefabrication
and mass production, approached them critically, but their
verdict, after a few voyages, was generally favourable.

Captain Houghton, who took over the *Samderwent* from the
builders at Portland, Maine, had plenty of opportunity to
form his conclusions on a first all-round voyage which included a crossing of the North Atlantic and a double crossing
of the South Atlantic before his ship arrived in a home port.
Although a little technical, his views are worth recording.
"The side plating and decks of this vessel are all welded, with
the frames of 'Z' section riveted to the plating," he wrote.
"Deck beams are welded to plates. 286 tons of solid ballast
are stowed in the hold bilges, whilst the dry tank has been
filled with eighty tons of fresh water and sealed off. In bad
weather, this vessel rolls heavily, and this may be due in part
to the fact that the bilge keels are not welded throughout their
length to the ship's side, but have lengths of welding alternat-
ing with slots cut into the keel. When the vessel rolls, these
slots allow the water to pass from under the bilge keel to the
top without exerting any force to stop the rolling, and so
reduce the efficiency of the bilge keels. The navigating bridge
is very well fitted, but there are too many obstructions forward
to allow it to be used for safe navigation, especially in convoy.
The flying bridge, from which the watch is kept, has been
given some elementary protection round the wheel. A per-
manent wooden rail and dodger has been built by ship's staff
on the fore side of this bridge. . . . The compasses are satisfactory, but are rather sluggish owing to the proximity of so

much iron. . . . The vessel is fitted with two bower and one stream anchor only. There are 135 fathoms of cable on the port anchor and 75 on the starboard. There are no shackles, and the lengths of cable are connected with riveted links, so that chain cannot be unshackled for clearing hawse or mooring in ports such as Calcutta. There is no high frequency receiver in the wireless room, nor was a broadcast receiver installed. The ship is wired for these items and is also wired for a gyroscope compass. Ventilation to the accommodation is not good. Vents are fitted into the upper accommodation from the stokehold ventilators and are not satisfactory, flooding the alleyways in cold weather, and generally allowing more foul air from the stokehold into the accommodation than fresh air. Since plugging these vents the air has been much healthier. Apart from these points, the vessel is well fitted. She appears to be strong, and apart from a tendency to 'hog' when fully loaded, she has shown no signs of weakness."

Captain Houghton concluded with an appreciative reference to the hot and cold water system fitted in the American-built ships. It had undoubtedly increased the cleanliness of the crew, he said, and a careful check of the quantities used disclosed that, with adjustment of pressure, no more water was used with the shower-bath system than with the older hand-pump system.

Although this was hardly an instance, there were occasions during the war when one was surprised by the ready acceptance of progressive American ideas by hard-bitten British sailors who might have been expected to regard them as "new-fangled". Going to clear the entrance to a Brittany harbour in a small American-built minesweeper towards the end of the war, I found she was commanded by a Skipper Lieutenant whose tough occupation in peace-time was deep-sea fishing.

In the little wardroom, the Americans had fitted a beautiful chromium-plated electric coffee percolator. Far from being despised, this luxury article was the Skipper's show-piece. Coffee trickled through it at all hours of the day and night and anyone asking for a cup of tea was regarded as nothing less than a heretic.

Another Portland-built ship, the *Samdon*, came under the command of the much-experienced Captain Crellin as soon as she was completed. After a few short trials, the vessel loaded in New York and then "behaved remarkably well" on a maiden voyage of 4,277 miles to Mediterranean ports. Captain Crellin noted that the ship's shell plating was riveted to the frames, with the butts flush and welded. She differed slightly from the Baltimore ships. Although she crossed the Atlantic again and then sailed to India before making her first appearance in the Clyde, Captain Crellin had no complaints. The *Samdon*, he said, had a speed of eleven knots loaded and twelve knots in ballast.

The *Sampenn* saw some lively action and plenty of ocean before Captain T. W. Ellis brought her into the Clyde. It was on her second run through the Mediterranean with supplies from the United States that she became involved in a minor sea-air battle. The *Sampenn* was sailing in a big Allied convoy on which the enemy made a determined attack with thirty planes. The first aircraft to come within range of the *Sampenn's* guns had a warm reception. It was sighted forward of the port beam, flying low at an estimated range of 1,500 yards. The 4-inch gun and all the port oerlikons went into action at once. The latter fired 180 rounds, and the tracers indicated that the enemy aircraft was well in the line of fire. Twenty minutes later, five more aeroplanes were seen coming in low astern of the convoy, but these kept clear of the *Sampenn* and were the target of other vessels. Later it became known that none of the ships in the convoy was hit, while the enemy lost five aircraft.

Two of the Baltimore Sams, the *Samnebra* (Captain F. Cossar) and the *Samchess* (Captain S. S. Davidson), were both busily engaged for some months before coming to home waters. The *Samnebra* made no less than eight voyages to Italy from Alexandria, Algiers and Bone, during which she carried over 3,500 tons of ammunition and stores, 1,379 tanks and motor vehicles and more than a thousand military personnel. Not once was she engaged by the enemy. In the autumn of 1944 she took on a load of Churchill tanks and steamed without incident to London.

The round voyage of the *Samchess*, too, was an indication of the waning power of our enemies over an even wider field. A slight collision while at anchor almost under the shadow of the Statue of Liberty before setting forth on her first Atlantic crossing, might have been regarded as an omen of troublous times to come. But after a double crossing of the Atlantic and a visit to Calcutta and Colombo, Captain Davidson had nothing worse to report than some dirty south-west monsoon weather on the way from Aden to Colombo.

The handing over of these American-built ships to the British Ministry of War Transport often meant a quick change of name. Within a week of her launch at the Bethlehem Fairfield Shipyard as the S.S. *Israel Wheelen*, a 7,219-ton ship became the S.S. *Samport*. Her British Master, Captain MacMillan, took over, and a fortnight later the *Samport* was heading eastward in her first Atlantic convoy. Her cargo was discharged at Port Said after another twenty-six days, and the vessel steamed on to Kilindini. From there she went to Lourenço Marques where she was welcomed as the first British operated Liberty ship to enter the port.

Considerable use was being made at this time of the defence

nets which were a familiar feature of the Liberty ships. The *Sambrian* (Captain R. B. Linsley) streamed them for five consecutive days in the Mediterranean. They were streamed again after clearing the swept channel from Aden, and when they suffered damage it was considered of sufficient importance to divert the ship to Durban so that they could be renewed. The additional security offered by the nets was thought to justify the slight loss of speed entailed in towing them.

Although the Liberty ships came to take the place of the well-tried

> "ships that sailed for sunny isles,
> But never came to shore,"

there were still many well-known Clan-named vessels plying the majority, if not all, the Seven Seas. Home-comings over a period of six weeks to the end of October, 1944, began to build up a list of names such as might start off a Roll Call of the famous 51st Division. *Murray, Macgillivray, Macbean, Macdonald, Cameron, Macnair* and *Urquhart*—with Battle Honours between them which might be compared with those of the incomparable Highland Division—all came sailing in. And what had their Masters got to say of their long voyages after five years of war? Here and there a "high spot" came in for special description, but four-fifths of what they set on record was in such phrases as: "Outward passage in convoy —seven knots—was slow," "Leaky tubes developed in the port boiler and the boiler was shut down and six tubes plugged," "The weather for the first few days was bad, the northerly gales persisting, and we took on a heavy list of 12 degrees to port owing to the slag ballast shifting," "Coal burned included Welsh, Natal and Indian. The Welsh was good and the other two fairly good steaming," "Vessel is now nearly eleven months out of dry dock and her bottom is dirty," "Buoys were sighted up to No. 24, but at midnight sea turned calm with dense fog which lasted until next morning when No. 30 buoy was sighted," "I am sorry to report that they could not sell the sand ballast for building purposes," "Machinery throughout the voyage has been very satisfactory. There has been perfect combustion from fuel, and an entire absence of smoke," "Passage was uneventful."

The last remark applied to most of the passages in the eyes of the Masters who, through the years, had seen so much. Captain Watkinson, of the *Macnair*, was prepared to say that a passage from west to east across the Atlantic was "without incident", although here is his own description of the departure of the convoy from the United States: "The Convoy Conference took place the next morning ashore, and seventy-eight ships were represented. My time for departure was given for just after 10 p.m. and I was under weigh at 10.18 p.m. and got into line for proceeding down channel. It was a beautiful starry night on leaving, but half-way down channel a heavy snow blizzard came on with a strong north-westerly wind. For the rest of the night visibility was reduced to nil and until well into the following morning nothing was seen. I kept on the course and speed ordered for the convoy, and when the weather cleared I was fortunate to be in sight of the Commodore. The escort were kept busy for the rest of the day rounding up the ships of the convoy, and we ended up by carrying on with fifty-eight ships instead of seventy-eight."

After that testing start, the convoy, which had a very powerful escort of twenty-eight ships—the crossing was made during the D-Day build-up period—enjoyed an unmolested, fine weather passage. Thirty vessels entered the Mediterranean, where the escort was reduced to four corvettes. "We sailed close to the North African shore to Cape Bon, then south of Pantelleria, north of Malta and then close to the coast of

Cyrenaica," the Master of the *Macnair* recorded. "Off this coast, when we were passing a westbound convoy, the ships were attacked by about eight German aircraft. It was in the middle of the night but the convoy was lit up by the full moon and parachute flares which were dropped. Intense anti-aircraft fire was put up by the ships and we had the pleasure of seeing one German plane coming down in flames. No ships of either convoy were hit or suffered damage."

The word "uneventful" returned to the Master's account when describing the Aden-Colombo leg of his voyage, although he mentioned that an American ship, which had been in company with the *Macnair* crossing the Atlantic, was torpedoed north of Minikoi in a position the *Macnair* had passed only ten hours earlier.

Two fast Clan ships, the *Cameron* and *Campbell*, were chosen to go with an impressive convoy that sailed east from this country a month or so after D-Day. They were in the company of such "ladies" as the *Strathnaver*, *Strathaird*, *Empress of Australia*, *Orion*, *Queen of Bermuda* and *Mooltan*. The Clan ships found no difficulty in maintaining speeds that gave an average of fourteen knots over the whole passage to Port Said. The best day's run gave an average of 15.2 knots for twenty-four hours. Captain Hardinge, of the *Cameron*, found the newly installed Radar of great use in keeping station during fog. The *Cameron* carried explosives both out and home. Her voyage continued to Bombay, where she was allowed to dock when she was down to about 2,000 tons of explosives. The engineers were unable to carry out a boiler and machinery overhaul, however, because the authorities insisted that the ship should have main steam ready to shift the vessel at a moment's notice. No sooner was she empty than the loading of 15-inch naval shells began.

Although the authorities were obviously nervous after the

big explosion in the Victoria dock—about a dozen wrecked or burnt-out vessels were still sitting on the bottom of the waterless dock—fines which Captain Hardinge regarded as "quite inadequate" were imposed when three men, who had been caught smoking in the ship by sabotage watchers, were charged. One man was actually smoking in the hold among the explosives, but the Court's decision in each case was "Five rupees or one day's imprisonment."

One more example of masterly conciseness can be presented in a twelve-line report from Captain Herbert J. Giles, which not only covered the voyage of the *Clan Urquhart* to New Zealand, but dealt with a startling encounter. Captain Giles wrote: "We sailed independently from the Mersey, a full ship, on the afternoon of July 12. Good weather was experienced to Panama, where we arrived on the morning of July 27, making an average of sixteen knots from Liverpool. The only incident of the passage was the night we passed through the Mona Channel (West Indies) when a submarine cut very close across our stem. On arrival in Colon, I was informed that three tankers had been torpedoed within the last few days in the Caribbean Sea, so presume it was an enemy craft passing out into the Atlantic. After completing with oil fuel, I entered the Canal on the morning of July 28, and passed into the Pacific and proceeded on my voyage at 5 p.m. the same day. On August 16, I arrived Auckland. Several days of heavy weather were experienced during the voyage. Average speed 15.46 knots."

The one war route not much frequented by Clan ships was the unpleasant one carrying the supply line to North Russia. Most men who went that way will agree, I think, that the weather was more often than not a harder enemy to face than the Huns perched menacingly around the North Cape. A mid-winter journey with the Commandos as far as the Lofoten

*Christmas 1945. "The Clan Cameron"
arrived in the Royal Victoria Dock, London
in her peacetime colours.*

Islands gave me a sample of the hardships inflicted by climatic conditions alone. Even the Commando men, trained to swim through icy mountain streams in Scotland, were provided with string vests, oiled socks, heavy woollen jerseys and special wind-resisting suits for operations in this area. With spray turning to ice as it broke over the bows of ships, one learned to fear exposure more than any other mischance.

In the early winter of 1944, one of the Liberty ships, the *Adolph S. Ochs*, sailed from Manchester and joined a north-bound convoy. Once again the Master, Captain E. W. Jenkin, could use the word "uneventful" for both the outward and return voyages. His ship was in North Russian waters for more than five weeks from the time she arrived at Kola Inlet. Sailing in latitudes above sixty-five degrees north, he found that the magnetic compasses became unreliable. The *Adolph S. Ochs* discharged her cargo in Archangel, suffering a buckled derrick while landing aeroplane parts weighing nearly three tons. A cargo of pit props was loaded for the return voyage which was safely concluded in a belated northerly gale.

If the turn-round of the *Adolph S. Ochs* was a long-drawn-out process, the *Clan Macdougall* was suffering even more aggravating delays at about the same time on the other side of the world. Diverted from her route on the latter part of a voyage to Sydney, she was instructed to put in to a bay which her Master (Captain H. M. Rodger) had never heard of and for which he had no charts. Informed of this, the authorities made a signal telling Captain Rodger to proceed to point "Charlie" on his original course, where he would receive fresh instructions. The *Macdougall* spent twenty-six hours in the area of point "Charlie" before a Dutch coastal steamer came out and led her, and an American tanker, towards the coast. A pilot boarded the tanker, but after arriving in Milne Bay he asked the *Macdougall* not to follow his movements further.

Captain Rodger began a cautious search for the unknown Stringer Bay. After a time he made contact with a signal station and asked: "Where is Stringer Bay?" The answer, which he no doubt received with a mixture of irritation and relief, was: "Right here."

Captain Rodger presumed that twenty-three landing-craft were to be put ashore at this point, but when the shore authorities made their first contact with him next day he was only given his route instructions to the next port and told that a floating-crane would come alongside. Another thirty hours went by and then a polite signal from the shore asked the irate Master: "When do you intend to unload boats?" In reply, Captain Rodger asked when it was proposed to send the floating-crane and labour. Twenty hours later, with the floating-crane still not alongside, he made the blunt signal: "Understand this vessel is urgently required in Australia. When are we to commence discharge barges?" The answer to this was a request to move to a new position from which it was possible for the waiting crew of the *Macdougall* to see the floating-crane lying idle at a jetty!

More signals were exchanged but it was not until another fifteen wasted hours had slipped by that the crane arrived. After unloading, four of the landing-craft were left lying unattended alongside all night. They were finally moved after Captain Rodger had made an urgent signal saying that he could hold up his sailing no longer and the craft would be cast adrift if they were not taken over at once. Such lack of co-operation, fortunately, was quite exceptional.

As our battle line in Europe swept forward, there were many manifestations at sea that the long awaited end was not far off. The Master of the *Clan Ranald*, homeward bound after an eight months' voyage, echoed the immortal words of Browning in his own phlegmatic way when he said: "It was quite exciting seeing Cape St. Vincent once again after avoiding such well-known headlands for so many years." And surely the Master, and thousands more, had given the answer to

> " 'Here and here did England help me: how can I help England?'
>   —say,
> Whoso turns as I, this evening, turn to God to praise and pray,
> While Jove's planet rises yonder, silent over Africa."

As early as mid-November, 1944, Captain Lofthouse sailed independently through the Mediterranean in the *Clan Campbell* with navigation lights burning. He agreed with Captain Storkey, of the *Clan Farquhar*, who sailed from Aden to Suez with lights on for the first time since the outbreak of war, that things were really getting back to normal. Still, Captain Storkey was a little disturbed to find that the convoy he joined at Gibraltar had only one escort ship assigned to it. If this created a suspicion that events were moving faster than many could appreciate, the scene on the arrival of the *Clan Farquhar* in this country must have provided confirmation. Coming into St. Helen's Roads, off the Isle of Wight, after darkness had fallen, the Master of the 8,000-ton merchant ship, who had been away since before D-Day, was amazed at the immense activity. "On approaching the anchorage the position became so confused, with naval craft under way with green and red lights all over them, that I deemed it safer to anchor for the time being," he wrote later. Delayed by fog, the *Farquhar* eventually arrived in the Alexandra Dock, Hull, on Christmas Eve.

On the same day, in far away Vizagapatam, Madras, Captain Coultas and his Engineer Officers were being relieved after voyaging for more than twenty months in the M.V. *Empire Elaine*. During that time they had served Combined Operations at the Sicily landings, had been on special service in the Indian Ocean, had carried an 85-ton tug and many landing-craft to ports in the Eastern war zone, had run through the monsoon, taken part in the South of France landings and had then returned for further service in Indian waters. All of which was reported in matter of fact form by Captain Coultas with hardly a personal reference beyond his final words: "I shall report myself to you on my arrival in the United Kingdom."

When Captain Watkinson brought the *Bangkok II* home early in 1945, he had an amusing and in no way disrespectful story to tell of an unexpected distinction conferred on his ship during her voyage. Captain Watkinson had taken over the command of the *Bangkok II* at Durban owing to the illness of Captain S. F. Carter. Among the items loaded into the ship was a somewhat mysterious case boldly marked "Natural History Specimen". It was consigned to the Persian Embassy in Cairo, and the British Master soon discovered that he was in fact carrying the embalmed body of the ex-Shah of Persia. The case was carefully stowed, and for the next month Captain Watkinson was probably more concerned with a consignment of mustard gas, which was being guarded on board by a small party of military personnel, than he was with the "specimen".

But on the day before the *Bangkok II* was due to arrive at Suez he received a wireless message from the naval authorities saying: "Please confirm expected time of arrival—also whether one case marked 'Natural History Specimen', stowed No. 3 shelter, available immediate discharge." He replied: "Time arrival 0400. 'Natural History Specimen', stowed No. 3 shelter, available discharge after removal small quantity rubber tyres."

At daylight next day an Examination Officer arrived on board. He told the Master, not without an air of importance, that when he arrived at his anchorage in Suez Bay he was not to be alarmed if he heard gunfire. The body of the ex-Shah of Persia was expected to arrive in the port and a salute of twenty-one guns would be fired.

Let the rest of the story be told in Captain Watkinson's quite inimitable words: "The Examination Officer was nothing short of astounded when I told him the guns would not go off until I arrived as I had the body on board! Anchoring at 8.48 a.m., the ship was boarded immediately by the Port Captain and officers of the Egyptian Navy, who had come to prepare for the ceremony that was to take place. The rubber tyres were soon removed and the case landed on deck. Then I was asked questions such as: 'Can you guarantee the body is in that case?' and 'At which end of the case is the head?' I told them I could not answer these questions. The case was then draped with a large Persian Ensign and, at a given signal, a tug came alongside with the Persian Ensign at half-mast. The Admiral in charge of King Farouk's yacht came on board. The case was then put on to the tug and ten Egyptian sailors acted as bodyguard. The tug left the ship's side followed by several launches, making quite an impressive sight. As I masted our Ensign, so the gun at Tewfik 'roared' out its salute. Time on passage Aden to Suez, 6 days 16 hours 19 minutes. Average speed 8.43 knots. Total distance 1,337 miles. Coal consumed 333 tons."

The excellent work of another Sam ship, the *Samaye*, which arrived in home waters for the first time in February, 1945, must be noted. Under her Master, Captain A. V. Gordon, who had sailed with his crew to America in the liner *Queen Elizabeth* to take over the new vessel, she had completed no less than eight voyages on the shuttle supply run between the United States and Italy. Her cargo summary for these voyages was: Government stores, motor transport and ammunition, 13,709 tons; petrol in drums and jerricans, 28,390 tons. The

Samaye had experienced a few air raids and one submarine attack, but there was another threat which received special comment from Captain Gordon. "Navigation on the Italian coast calls for great care as minefields are extensive and potent," he wrote. "We have seen many mines near the vessel and a number of ships have been mined."

Ports whose names had not come into the logs of British ships for years were once again appearing in the records. The *Samaye* paid a visit to Antwerp, and the *Empire Forest* (Captain Pengelly) went right up the river to Morlaix to delight the French people with some precious coffee. Having been present at the early stages of mine clearance in the rugged entrance to this French port, I can endorse Captain Pengelly's comment: "Morlaix is not by any means an easy port to make, owing to shoals and rocks extending well off-shore. Ships must moor bow and stern to buoys in the harbour and they have not sufficient room to swing at low water."

Chapter Twelve

"Whom Fate Can Never Surprise"

The merchant seaman never faltered. He sailed voyage
after voyage, perhaps on occasions changing the North
Atlantic for North Russia or for Malta. To him we owe
our preservation and our very lives.

ALFRED BARNES,
MINISTER OF WAR TRANSPORT, SEPTEMBER, 1945

IN MARCH, 1945, WHEN WE ENTERED THE TWELFTH AND LAST
half-year of war, the grand finale was in sight. Events moved
forward with a rapidity that made it difficult for those on shore
to keep abreast of them, and were almost beyond the powers
of digestion of those still serving on the high seas. In less than
a month, there came news that the Navy had helped Field-
Marshal Montgomery's 21st Army Group to force the Rhine
on a 25-mile front north of the Ruhr, that the Russians had
captured the port and naval base of Gdynia, that a large
convoy had reached Murmansk without loss and that powerful units of the British Pacific Fleet had joined in attacks on
the Ryukyu Islands as a preliminary to the invasion of
Okinawa.

It was clear from the world-wide nature of the operations
designed to smash the enemy once and for all, that shipping
remained of the utmost importance to the Allies. In an all-out
effort, British ships ran supplies from America to help support
the Armies in the East, while American ships, and those of

many other nationalities, joined with ours in serving the forces that battered their way into Germany on two sides. Captain Simpson, making his way down Channel in the *Clan Macbean*, noted Norwegian, Dutch, Belgian and Swedish vessels in the convoy.

The North Russia convoy mentioned had again included the *Adolph S. Ochs*, and Captain Jenkin, arriving in the Orkney Islands on March 31, had a story to tell which left no doubt that Merchant Navy men were still in the forefront of the battle. The northbound convoy, of which he was Vice-Commodore, sailed at the beginning of February. It was twice attacked by large formations of German torpedo-bombers, but the escort, which included aircraft-carriers, was more than equal to each occasion. There were no casualties among the ships of the convoy, but at least eight enemy aeroplanes were shot down. The Master of the *Adolph S. Ochs* ("Adolph's Socks", to the sailors), became Commodore of the White Sea section of the convoy. Two pilots were picked up from the icebreaker *Stalin* at the ice-edge. Following in the wake of the *Stalin*, the British merchantman still had to grind her way through ice which varied in thickness from one to four feet. One huge chunk badly bent a blade of her propeller and reduced her speed by two knots. Some of the ship's cargo was taken out at Molotovsk and she then proceeded to Archangel, towed by the icebreaker *Northwind*. The damaged propeller was examined and the Surveyor declared that when navigating in ice it must be submerged not less than 25 feet 3 inches, which was cold comfort to Captain Jenkin as the deepest draught allowed to cross the bars in the Dvina river was 22 feet 6 inches, and he was still above them. Nevertheless, after ten days of anxious sailing through the white bleakness, the *Adolph S. Ochs* left the edge of the ice on March 23 and completed the round trip in a succession of southerly gales.

Arriving in home waters about the same time after a voyage in very different climes—he had been to Australia and New Zealand—Captain Giles, in the *Clan Urquhart*, reported a number of submarines in the vicinity of the convoy. Again our strength was proved. One U-boat was sunk and the convoy was not even attacked. The *Clan Campbell*, also from the other side of the world, came in with a number of troopships returning from the Mediterranean. She carried in addition to general cargo, 1,234 bags of mail.

The *Clan Macdonald* was one of the ships engaged in transporting supplies directly from the United States to the American forces in the Australasian zone. She sailed from New York to New Guinea, via the Panama Canal, and Captain Cater was able to give a most interesting account of developments in what remained a remote theatre of war for most of us. "I was greatly struck by all the amenities existing in New Guinea ports, considering the short time they have been in existence," he wrote. "Taking Hollandia and Imri, which had only been occupied by the Americans since the previous April, as examples—there were eleven deep-water wharves. Fresh water, which could be delivered at sixty tons an hour, was laid on; there were floating-cranes of up to eighty tons capacity, floating dry-docks and a number of repair ships. On shore there were excellent roads properly policed (the traffic was terrific both by day and by night), street lighting, cinemas and theatres, broadcasting stations, three daily papers, petrol pumps by the wayside, and a café run by the American Red Cross with outside tables shaded by gaily coloured umbrellas. U.S. Government vessels of all sizes, from a large tug upwards, all seemed to have their own cinemas and washing-machines. Last, but not least, there was a mail delivery from the United States every third day—average time of transit, five days! Amusements were free, as also was postage by airgraph to the United States. All

199

this, I was informed, would shortly be abandoned as being too far behind the scene of operations. . . ."

The greatest war in history was indeed sweeping on to its triumphant conclusion for the Allies. The scene had changed almost beyond belief during one round voyage of the S.S. *Lieut. St. Loubert Bie.* Sailing from Birkenhead in mid-November, 1943, she had been in ports too numerous to mention before she returned to this country in April, 1945. During that period, the splendid contribution towards victory of the ship commanded by Captain H. T. Booth can be summed up in three bold lines:

Total distance steamed, 55,736 miles.
Total cargo handled, 90,000 tons.
Average speed, 10 knots.

But even at this late hour not all Masters were to have the happy satisfaction of celebrating the victory they had striven so mightily to bring about. Captain Stormont, confined to his cabin in the *Samaye*, outward bound for New York, thought that he had bad indigestion and declared that he would be fit again next day. But he suddenly became seriously ill and died before medical assistance could be obtained from other vessels in the convoy. With the Commodore, and the Masters and crews of fine ships paying their respects across the grey Atlantic, Captain Stormont went to his final resting-place while, for a brief interval, his ship was stilled and his crew heard the new Master, Captain Blackwell, read the Burial Service.

Ships came and went, and it was fitting that the great majority should be at sea when the announcement of the long-awaited victory in Europe was made on May 8. Many of them were sailing singly again through familiar waters, with memory alone charting the exploits of more than sixty months of war. Let us find a few of these ships, gallant survivors of the worst a strong and barbarous nation could do at the second attempt in a quarter of a century.

Three stalwarts, the *Buteshire*, the *Clan Macneil* and the *Clan Macilwraith*, were meeting in Mombasa harbour. The *Buteshire* had been in for two days, coming from Dar-es-Salaam; the *Macneil* for longer, and the *Macilwraith*, outward bound, came in in the early evening and anchored in the harbour because there was no berth available. What form the victory celebrations took I cannot say, the Masters only referring to the occasion in their subsequent reports in order to account for two days of public festivity when no work was done in their ships. The *Clan Chisholm* was well on her way to Calcutta and the *Clan Macaulay* was in Sydney.

The *Samdon* was busy getting clear of a south-west gale that had brought her speed down to four knots as she approached the South American coast. The *Sampenn* was entering the inner harbour at Brindisi and the *Clan Ranald* was just heading up to Aden. The *Clan Maciver* was beating across the Pacific from New Zealand at a steady ten knots and the *Clan Cameron* was entering the Indian Ocean on an outward voyage. The *Clan Colquhoun* had just paid a visit to Pitcairn Island to deliver mail, and three lucky men out of twelve more or less marooned on the island, were taking passage in her to Auckland. Captain Hogg's chief preoccupation on V.E. Day was with a defect that caused the port engine to be shut in to forty-five revolutions. The *Adolph S. Ochs* was preparing for another run into the Arctic and the *Empire Prince*, a visitor to Piræus three months earlier, was awaiting a berth at Beira.

The *Clan Macbean* was steaming through the Mediterranean when she received a wireless message from the C.-in-C.,

Mediterranean Fleet, conveying the news of the forthcoming surrender of Germany and paying tribute to the work of both the Royal Navy and the Merchant Navy. At Gibraltar she had been told by signal that navigation lights could be shown at full brilliancy and the black-out was no longer necessary. Her log, summarised, as she steamed eastward, was:

May 5: 8 a.m., off Oran.

May 6: 3 a.m., off Algiers. 8 a.m., signalled C. Guardia.

May 7: 10 a.m., off Bizerta. 6 p.m., passed Pantellaria. 8 p.m., received W/T message that war in Europe would be officially declared over the following day.

May 8: 2.30 a.m., passed Malta. 8 a.m., Ensigns and House flags hoisted in celebration of V.E. Day and crew given a holiday, except men necessary for duty. Received following message W/T from Admiralty: "The German High Command has been directed to give the following Orders to U-boats: (a) To remain on the surface flying a large black or blue flag. (b) To make for specified ports under Allied control. (c) To report their position in plain language on 505 kcs. every eight hours. U-boats apparently complying with these instructions are not to be attacked, but should be given a wide berth. Reports of such sightings are to be made in plain language in the following form: (a) Number of U-boat. (b) Position. (c) Estimated course. (d) Speed. If, however, U-boats commit a hostile act or otherwise disregard these orders, report is to be made by normal distress procedure and all appropriate defence measures taken." 3 p.m., received following W/T message from Admiral, Alexandria: "Clan Macbean enter Alexandria, repeat Alexandria."

May 9: Crew, except men on duty, given holiday this day also, to comply with home celebrations.

May 10: Received W/T message from Lord Leathers,

Minister of War Transport, giving thanks to Merchant Navy for their share in victory over Germany.

May 11: 11.13 a.m., entered Alexandria swept channel.

So the Mediterranean ceased to be "a sea of conflict", and became again a great natural artery of trade and commerce between East and West. Here, and in the Atlantic, the fundamental nature of sea power had been proved up to the hilt. It was something that many Nazis, vaingloriously absorbed with the early successes of the German armies, failed to appreciate until defeat had overtaken their oppressive cause. The situation has been most aptly described by the German naval officer already mentioned who played an important part in the Mediterranean war, Vice-Admiral Weichold, chief Naval Liaison Officer at Rome and Flag Officer, German Naval Command, Italy, 1940–43. "The war," he wrote, after the conclusion of hostilities, "being a world war, was intrinsically a naval war. It should therefore have been conducted [by the Germans] from the ocean-maritime point of view, no matter how small the navy or how great the army and the air force were as war factors."

The continental outlook was the dominating factor in the Reich's policy. "For this reason," he continued, "in future the natural land-bound outlook of the Germans must be broadened to grasp a more far-reaching and general relation to world problems. The sea is the best teacher for this. In contrast to the land, with its narrow territorial, material and spiritual boundaries, the sea is the great element that binds the peoples together. It is common to all, everybody's road. It demonstrates that the nations form one community, that they are interdependent, that co-operation, respect and considerateness are necessary, and thus it encourages a feeling of community. Without wishing to misunderstand or alter the national foundations of the peoples, the sea is nevertheless, with its work of education, the highest class in the school of mankind. It broadens one's thinking, frees it from the restrictions of partiality, and leads to a comprehensive view of the life of men and nations. Such education has as its result a development of individualism, which leads to the further development of democratic principles. It is an unquestionable fact that amongst all peoples individualistic and democratic achievements have developed from a way of life connected with the sea and seafaring. The value of the sea within the framework of man's development is one of the greatest experiences of the lost war."

Wise but belated words: if this lesson could have been brought home to Hitler and his supporters *before* 1939, the whole course of history might have been altered.

Seen through British eyes, it was startlingly clear that without sea-power there could be no survival. Let one of our own Admirals, Rear-Admiral R. K. Dickson, D.S.O., repeat the words he used in a broadcast on Trafalgar Day, 1945. "We British have once again been delivered out of the hands of our enemies; and surely for *us* the fundamental lesson of the last six years is still the old one which has been taught us by all our wars. It's this, that in the whole changing kaleidoscope of war there's one constant factor—the simple merchant ship—and that for as long as we remain an island at the heart of a maritime Empire our survival depends on being able to protect the merchant ship against *anything* an enemy can do. The invention of new explosives, of the aeroplane, the submarine, the long-range gun, right back to the invention of gunpowder—nothing *new* has ever altered that fundamental lesson, because the chief purpose of these things in the hands of our enemies has always been to obstruct the passage of the merchant ship across the sea. The sole purpose of British sea power has been to secure safe passage for our own merchant ships and to deny it to the enemy, and the result has always been decisive. Hitler learnt what it meant, first to be throttled by the thin ring of sea power which was thrown round Europe, and then to have his flanks torn open by it. So did the Kaiser and Napoleon and Louis XIV and Philip of Spain."

. . . . .

The *coup de grâce* still had to be administered to Japan, and war had first call on shipping for another three months. It may be said that as far as de-control was concerned, peace took over where war left off, and the return to normal sailing conditions proved to be a very slow business.

We will follow the *Clan Forbes*, the ship we set out with in 1939, through these final and transitional months. Her tenth voyage, completed in January, 1945, had been marked by heavy delays owing to the congested state of ports in the East. With rain also interfering with the discharge of cargo, she had spent two months in Colombo. She sailed to Suez with over 100,000 cubic feet of the cargo spaces filled with tea for the British Army.

The eleventh voyage took her through the Mediterranean independently at an average speed of 14.7 knots, which would have been improved upon if Captain Andrews had not reduced speed over the last twelve hours in order to enter Port Said in daylight. Routeing instructions were received at Aden, and the *Forbes* arrived safely first in Karachi and then in Bombay. Her return cargo was 1,000 tons of linseed, loaded at Bombay, and 6,000 tons of groundnuts, 1,000 tons of castor seed and 115 tons of bone meal, loaded at Marmagoa. Filled to capacity, the big ship even had six tons of groundnuts stowed under the forecastle-head to complete shipment. She sailed home in just over three weeks. V.E. Day was a little more than a week away when the *Clan Forbes* made her last coastal run in home waters under war conditions. There was no joy in it for Captain Andrews. Unfavourable weather conditions compelled him to carry on the pilot from Southend to Hull. "A strong north-west gale was encountered, and what with slow ships and most erratic station-keeping, innumerable buoys and sandbanks, and strong tides, it was quite an effort to avoid collision or running aground," he reported.

V.E. Day had been celebrated before the *Clan Forbes* set off on Voyage 12. V.J. Day was to be a thing of the past before she returned. It was fitting that this last voyage that we shall follow—but not the last by many that she will successfully accomplish, it is to be hoped—should be another normal routine run to Indian ports. She was oiling at Suez at the end of June. A night unloading of ten L.C.B.s, which had been carried on deck, took place on July 9. She was in Calcutta a week later, and in the middle of the Indian Ocean on her return trip when V.J. Day came. Her cargo on this occasion was consigned to French ports, and Captain Andrews no doubt reflected that the mess of war is not cleared up by the declarations that end hostilities. Both in Le Havre and Boulogne his fine ship came into contact with submerged objects, fortunately without damage being done to her.

. . . . .

There is not a great deal more to be written about these last war-time sailings. Even V.J. Day—or Victory in the Pacific Day as many seamen preferred to call it—brought little immediate change in the courses followed by big merchant ships. After all fighting ceased, there was still the same number of mouths to feed in the armies spread around the world. There were still minefields, too, and the wrecks in harbours and shallow waters which confined Masters to swept and controlled channels such as they had become used to over the

years. One concession was made after only a week or two—
the darkness of war was lifted. On a three-day voyage from
Hobart to Lyttelton, the end of which coincided with V.J.
Day, the *Clan Urquhart* followed a precise route and a strict
black-out was enforced. The black-out regulations had not been
relaxed when she sailed on to Wellington, but soon after she
left that port for Panama the message was received: "Ships
whether sailing in convoy or independently are not to zig-zag
and guns need not be manned. Navigation lights are to be
burned at full brilliancy and black-out regulations are cancelled." "After receiving this message the *Clan Urquhart* was
immediately lit up," Captain Parfitt reported with satisfaction.

He had previously made reference to another problem that
was to remain for a long time—that of the removal and disposal
of the piled-up sinews of war. At Sydney, "terribly congested,
with ships two abreast at every landing stage," he had found
"so much ammunition that they do not know what to do with
it". Much of it was "big ship stuff", and the *Clan Urquhart* herself carried 3,300 tons of the heaviest shells used by the Navy.

Arriving in home waters nearly three months after the
cessation of hostilities in Europe, the *Clan Macneil*, waiting
for the fog to clear off Great Ormes Head, was not far from
a floating mine. Such hazards were still very present for the
sailor, although it would have been more than ironic if anything untoward had happened to the *Macneil* at that stage of a
voyage which had been made without mishap over 34,680
miles of sea.

It would be unfair to say that, with the passing of war,
more attention was given to the elements by those who follow
the great calling of the sea. War had superimposed its dangers
on those which must always be counted a part of life at sea.
The unending struggle with the elements—sometimes fierce
and sometimes so slight as to be hardly noticeable—had gone

on as usual. Weather, it has been said, provides the people of Britain with an unfailing topic of conversation. For British seamen, sailing their ships in all known seas, it provides a constant challenge, only to be met in a spirit of unflagging determination and courage. Few can be remote from the sea in our small island, and when storms rage many are the prayers and thoughts that go forth for "those in peril on the sea". But there are other tests for those who make their livelihood in ships, and often they may not be appreciated by the landsman. Take, for instance, the *Clan Cameron* coming through the Red Sea for her first peace-time homing in six years. For those with duties on deck there was the constant irritation of fine sand wafted from the land by the hot wind. There was dense fog for a time and the temperature was never below the nineties. And for those below, let Captain Hardinge speak: "During the hottest part of the passage I went with the Chief Engineer round the engine-room, tunnel, boiler-room and dynamo flat. The temperature in the latter stood at 154 degrees fahrenheit. Certain parts of the engine-room were not a great deal below." Here men faced the intense and exhausting test of heat with the same hardihood displayed by thire comrades in the Arctic convoys against numbing cold.

The men who have to meet these hardships regard them as part of the day's work. They are grateful for the improved living conditions in modern ships, and see themselves as well off compared with some others. From Aden, in the very last week of the war, Captain Townrow sailed the *Clan Ranald* to a little-heard-of spot—Safaga. And this is what he wrote: 'It was my first visit to Safaga and it impressed upon me how very much we owe to such handfuls of men as those I found there. They are truly outposts of the Empire, for Safaga is just desert and barren rock with not a sign of green anywhere. During our stay, the temperature was round about 98 degrees day and night, and we were all very happy to get away in order to obtain at least some slight movement in the air."

Captain Jenkin and the crew of the *Adolph S. Ochs* must have welcomed the place in the sun that came to them after their voyages round the North Cape. From New York, where her torpedo-net booms were removed, she sailed to Bari, via Gibraltar, with 7,200 tons of general cargo. V.J. Day came as she steamed through the warm Mediterranean, and her next voyage took her to sun-baked South American ports.

Steaming up the Bristol Channel in a full gale more than six years after the outbreak of hostilities, the *Buteshire* cleared the minefield off Hartland Point and was then forced to heave-to for forty-eight hours until the weather moderated. It was the weather that called for lengthy comment from Captain Woodall after his ship, stout survivor of two wars, had safely docked at Swansea. Of other hazards he only said: "Several floating mines were sighted during the passage but they were never near enough to endanger the vessel in any way."

Ten days before Christmas, 1945, the *Clan Cameron* arrived in the Royal Victoria Dock, London, in her peace-time colours. Gone was the overall drab greyness of the long years of endurance. Once again the power and grace of the dark-painted hull was emphasised by the vivid white of the upper-works. The two bold splashes of colour on the funnel, matching the far-famed House flag, were new and bright. Only the fading Red Ensign remained to link visibly the present with the past.

And to the Merchant Navy that Christmastide went this message of greeting from His Majesty the King: "For six years we have kept this festival notwithstanding the darkness which overshadowed us and all the world; and now at last we celebrate it in peace and victory. It is at this moment, when the dangers and perils of war lie behind us, that we can best realise the full extent of your courage and steadfastness. We have been drawn very close together and have learned in how real a sense we are members one of another; it was our good fortune, in the many uncertainties which beset us, always to feel confident that you 'whom fate can never surprise nor death dismay', would fulfil whatever demands were made upon you, bringing us the materials for war and the food without which we should have perished. There are many who will make no more voyages, whose names and faces we shall remember with love and gratitude as we drink to absent friends. Many have already returned to their homes and families after long absence and perhaps have sailed again on more peaceful errands, and many more look forward to home-coming. Others are setting out for the first time to learn the great traditions of your service. To each one of you I wish all the blessings of peace and present happiness this Christmas."

Appendix

LIST OF AWARDS

The following decorations and awards were bestowed on members of the staffs of Clan Line Steamers and Associated Companies between
1939–1945

DECK DEPARTMENT

Captain, H. J. Giles, O.B.E.;
„   A Mackinlay, O.B.E.;
„   J. Vooght, O.B.E. and Mentioned in Gazette;
„   A. Campbell, O.B.E. and Mentioned in Gazette;
„   E. Coultas, O.B.E. and Lloyd's Medal;
„   E. Gough, O.B.E. and Mentioned in Gazette;
„   H. M. Rodger, O.B.E.;
„   C. D. Worthington, O.B.E.;
„   M. H. Jones, O.B.E.;
„   F. S. Lofthouse, O.B.E. and Lloyd's Medal;
„   F. B. Parker, O.B.E. and Mentioned in Gazette;
„   J. D. Matthews, O.B.E. and Mentioned in Gazette;
„   T. W. Inman, O.B.E.;
„   H. C. C. Simpson, O.B.E.;
„   R. Masters, Mentioned in Gazette;
„   J. H. Crellin, Mentioned in Gazette;
„   R. W. J. Bennet, Mentioned in Gazette;
„   J. McCrone, Mentioned in Gazette;
„   H. T. Booth, Commended.

Chief Officer, T. W. Ellis, M.B.E.;
    "   W. J. Jones, M.B.E.;
    "   L. C. Higgins, M.B.E.;
    "   J. J. Millar, M.B.E.;
    "   H. E. Carter, M.B.E.;
    "   F. D. Bonney, M.B.E. and Mentioned in Gazette;
    "   H. W. Chadd, M.B.E.;
    "   J. V. Findlay, Mentioned in Gazette;
    "   F. Cossar, Mentioned in Gazette.

Second Officer, W. J. Freestone, M.B.E.;
    "   A. H. Black, D.S.C.;
    "   F. C. Chisholm, Mentioned in Gazette;
    "   T. M. Rees-Davies, Mentioned in Gazette;
    "   R. H. McElligott, Mentioned in Gazette.

Third Officer, A. Mair, Mentioned in Gazette;
    "   J. H. Holman, Mentioned in Gazette;
    "   G. Andrews, Mentioned in Gazette;
    "   O. T. Roberts, Mentioned in Gazette.

Apprentice, A. G. Allson, D.S.M., and Lloyd's Medal;
    "   J. H. Wehner, B.E.M.;
    "   N. F. Wray-Cook, Mentioned in Gazette;
    "   R. H. Gollop, Commended;

Carpenter, G. E. Stanley, B.E.M.;
    "   F. H. Mullin, B.E.M.;
    "   R. Kelly, B.E.M.;
    "   J. Strain, B.E.M.;
    "   J. Cuthbert, B.E.M.;
    "   G. G. Anderson, B.E.M.;
    "   J. S. McLeod, Mentioned in Gazette.

Chief Steward, F. C. Titcombe, B.E.M.;
    "   D. C. Gibson, B.E.M.;
    "   R. Y. Taylor, Mentioned in Gazette;
    "   C. E. Smith, Mentioned in Gazette.

1st Radio Officer, R. F. Cole, M.B.E. and Mentioned in Gazette.

Gunner, R. McNeill, Mentioned in Gazette;
    ,,   J. M. Gilchrist, B.E.M.

LASCAR SEAMEN

Seacunny, Noor Hossien x Amir Hossien, B.E.M.;
Deck Serang, Mohomed x Abdulla, B.E.M., Mentioned in Gazette.
        11 Indian Seamen Mentioned in Gazette.

ENGINEERING DEPARTMENT

Chief Engineer, T. L. Main, O.B.E.;
      ,,   H. McLean, O.B.E.;
      ,,   J. R. Wilde, M.B.E.;
      ,,   W. Brown, O.B.E.;
      ,,   R. Hannah, O.B.E.;
      ,,   J. S. Cruickshank, O.B.E.;
      ,,   W. J. McCaughin, O.B.E.;
Chief Refrigerating Engineer, J. Drennan, M.B.E.;
Second Engineer, R. C. W. Bainbridge, M.B.E. and Lloyd's Medal;
      ,,   W. L. Braid, M.B.E.

Chief Engineer, N. M. Robertson, Mentioned in Gazette
Second Engineer, J. C. Marshall,   ,,
Fourth Engineer, W. McMurtrie,   ,,
Fifth Engineer, W. Cunningham   ,,
Chief Engineer, E. S. Eddisford,   ,,
Chief Refrigerating Engineer, J. M. Ruthven, Mentioned in Gazette and Lloyd's Medal
Chief Engineer, C. S. Currie, Mentioned in Gazette
      ,,   H. W. Spottiswood,   ,,

FATAL CASUALTIES

FATAL CASUALTIES TO CLAN LINE AND ASSOCIATED

COMPANIES SEAGOING PERSONNEL DURING SECOND WORLD WAR

Masters	6
Chief Officers	2
Second Officers	2
Third Officers	2
Fourth Officers	5
First Engineers	10
Second Engineers	5
Third Engineers	8
Fourth Engineers	7
Fifth Engineers	5
Sixth Engineers	4
Seventh Engineers	2
Eighth Engineer	1
Refrigerating Engineers	2
Electrician	1
Surgeons	3
Stewards	8
Radio Officers	16
Carpenters	5
Apprentices	6
M. N. Gunners and D.E.M.S. Ratings . . .	33
Indian, ratings	508
TOTAL .	641

APPENDIX

Clan Line, Scottish Shire Line and
Houston Line Fleets at Outbreak of War

CLAN LINE STEAMERS

NAME OF VESSEL	NATURE OF CASUALTY IF ANY	DATE	LOCATION	REMARKS
Clan Alpine	Torpedoed and sunk	13.3.43	N. Atlantic	
Clan Buchanan	Sunk by German Raider	28.4.41	Indian Ocean	
Clan Cameron				
Clan Campbell	Bombed and sunk	23.3.42	Off Malta	Aerial attack
Clan Chattan	Bombed and sunk	14.2.42	Mediterranean	
Clan Chisholm	Torpedoed and sunk	17.10.39	Atlantic	
Clan Colquhoun				
Clan Cumming	(1) Air attack	11.10.40	Liverpool	Vessel repaired
	(2) Sunk. Mined	15.4.41	Ægean Sea	
Clan Farquhar				
Clan Ferguson	Air attack	21.9.40	Alexandria	
	Sunk	12.8.42	Mediterranean	Aerial Torpedo
Clan Forbes	Bombed	16.8.40	London	Air attack Vessel repaired
Clan Fraser	Sunk after explosion	17.4.41	Ægean Sea Piræus	Air attack
Clan Lamont				
Clan Macalister	Bombed and sunk	29.15.40	Dunkirk	Air attack
Clan Macarthur	Torpedoed and sunk	12.8.43	Mozambique Channel	
Clan Macaulay	Bombed	19.1.41	Malta	Air attack Vessel repaired
Clan Macbean				
Clan Macbrayne				
Clan Macdonald				
Clan Macdougall	Torpedoed and sunk	31.5.41	Atlantic	
Clan Macfadyen	Torpedoed and sunk	26.11.42	Atlantic	
Clan Macfarlane	Sunk in collision	17.6.40	Indian Ocean	
Clan Macgillivray				
Clan Macilwraith				
Clan Macindoe	Lost after fire	27.4.43	Alexandria	Fire and stranding
Clan Macinnes	Damaged in aerial attack	5.41	Liverpool	Vessel repaired

APPENDIX

NAME OF VESSEL	NATURE OF CASUALTY IF ANY	DATE	LOCATION	REMARKS
Clan Maciver				
Clan Mackinlay	Bombed and sunk	6.11.40	North Sea	
Clan Macnab	Sunk. Collision in convoy	17.3.41	Atlantic	
Clan Macnair				
Clan Macnaughton	Torpedoed and sunk	1.8.42	Atlantic	
Clan Macneil				
Clan Macphee	Torpedoed and sunk	16.8.40	Atlantic	
Clan Macpherson	Torpedoed and sunk	1.5.43	Atlantic	
Clan Macquarrie	Torpedoed and sunk	13.6.42	Atlantic	
Clan Mactavish	Torpedoed and sunk	8.10.42	Off South African Coast	
Clan Macwhirter	Torpedoed and sunk	26.8.42	Atlantic	
Clan Matheson	Damaged in Japanese air attack	5/6.12.43	Calcutta	Vessel repaired
Clan Menzies	Torpedoed and sunk	29.7.40	Atlantic	
Clan Monroe	Mined and sunk	29.7.40	Thames Estuary	
Clan Morrison	Mined and sunk	24.2.40	North Sea	
Clan Murdoch				
Clan Murray				
Clan Ranald				
Clan Skene	Torpedoed and sunk	10.5.42	Atlantic	
Clan Stuart	Sunk. Collision in convoy	11.3.40	English Channel	

HOUSTON LINE STEAMERS

NAME OF VESSEL	NATURE OF CASUALTY IF ANY	DATE	LOCATION	REMARKS
Halizones	Bombed and sunk	30.7.43	Off Spain	
Harmodius	Torpedoed and sunk	8.3.43	Near Gibraltar	
Harmonides	Torpedoed and sunk	25.8.42	Indian Ocean	
Clan Ogilvy	Torpedoed	1940	Bay of Biscay	Vessel repaired
	Torpedoed and sunk	20.3.41	Atlantic	
Clan Ross	Torpedoed and sunk	2.4.42	Indian Ocean	

216